P9-EFG-628

MIDDLE EASTERN TERRORISM

THE ROOTS OF TERRORISM

MIDDLE EASTERN TERRORISM

T 31969

Arie Perliger

University of Haifa, Israel

Series Consulting Editors

Leonard Weinberg and William L. Eubank

University of Nevada, Reno

CHELSEA HOUSE
PUBLISHERS
An imprint of Infobase Publishing

Middle Eastern Terrorism

Copyright © 2006 by Infobase Publishing

All rights reserved. No part of this book may be reproduced or utilized in any form or by any means, electronic or mechanical, including photocopying, recording, or by any information storage or retrieval systems, without permission in writing from the publisher. For information contact:

Chelsea House
An imprint of Infobase Publishing
132 West 31st Street
New York NY 10001

Library of Congress Cataloging-in-Publication Data

Perliger, Arie.
   Middle Eastern terrorism /Arie Perliger.
      p. cm.—(The roots of terrorism)
   Includes bibliographical references and index.
ISBN 0-7910-8309-8 (hardcover)
   1. Terrorism—Middle East—Juvenile literature.
I. Title. II. Series.
HV6433.M5P47 2006
303.6'250956—dc22   2006006019

Chelsea House books are available at special discounts when purchased in bulk quantities for businesses, associations, institutions, or sales promotions. Please call our Special Sales Department in New York at (212) 967-8800 or (800) 322-8755.

You can find Chelsea House on the World Wide Web at http://www.chelseahouse.com

Series and cover design by Takeshi Takahashi

Printed in the United States of America

Bang 21C 10 9 8 7 6 5 4 3 2 1

This book is printed on acid-free paper.

All links and web addresses were checked and verified to be correct at the time of publication. Because of the dynamic nature of the web, some addresses and links may have changed since publication and may no longer be valid.

Leonard Weinberg and William L. Eubank
University of Nevada, Reno

Terrorism is hard to ignore. Almost every day television news shows, newspapers, magazines, and Websites run and re-run pictures of dramatic and usually bloody acts of violence carried out by ferocious-looking terrorists or claimed by shadowy militant groups. It is often hard not to be scared when we see people like us killed or maimed by terrorist attacks at fast food restaurants, in office buildings, on public buses and trains, or along normal-looking streets.

This kind of fear is exactly what those staging terrorist attacks hope to achieve. They want the public, especially the American public, to feel a profound sense of fear. Often the leaders of terrorist groups want the public not only frightened by the attack, but also angry at the government because it seems unable to protect them from these violent assaults.

This series of books for young people has two related purposes. The first is to place the events we see in context. We want young readers to know what terrorism is about: Who its perpetrators are, where they come from, and what they hope to gain by their violence. We also want to answer some basic questions about this type of violence: What is terrorism? What do we mean when we use the term? Is one man's terrorist another man's freedom fighter? Is terrorism new, a kind of asymmetrical warfare just invented at the beginning of the twenty-first century? Or, does terrorism have a long history stretching back over the centuries? Does terrorism ever end? Should we expect to face waves of terrorist violence stretching into the indefinite future?

This series' second purpose is to reduce the anxieties and fears of young readers. Getting a realistic picture of what terrorism is all about, knowing what is true and what is not true about it helps us "get a grip." Young readers will learn, we hope, what constitutes realistic concerns about the danger of terrorism versus irrational fear. By understanding the nature of the threat, we help defeat one of the terrorists' basic aims: spreading terror.

The first volume in the series, *What is Terrorism?*, by Leonard Weinberg and William L. Eubank, begins by defining the term "terrorism," then goes on to explain the immediate aims and long-term objectives of those who decide to use this unconventional form of violence. Weinberg and Eubank point out that terrorism did not begin with the 9/11 attacks on the United States. In fact, terrorist violence has a long history, one the authors trace from its religious roots in the ancient Middle East up to current times.

For those who believe that terrorist campaigns, once started, are endless, Jeffrey Ian Ross's *Will Terrorism End?* will come as a useful antidote. Ross calls our attention to the various ways in which terrorist episodes have ended in the past. Many readers will be surprised to learn that most of the terrorist organizations that were active in Latin America, Western Europe, and the United States just a few decades ago have passed from the scene. For example, the Irish Republican Army (IRA), long active in paramilitary operations in Northern Ireland, is now in the process of turning to peaceful political participation.

Between accounts of the beginning and end of terrorism are books that approach the problem in two different ways. Dipak K. Gupta (*Who are the Terrorists?*) and Assaf Moghadam (*The Roots of Terrorism*) answer general questions about the origins of terrorists and terrorist organizations. Gupta provides profiles of individual terrorists and terrorist groups, in addition to exploring the issues that inspire terrorists. Moghadam, on the other hand, is more concerned with the organizational and social roots of terrorism. For example: What causes people to join terrorist groups? What are the grievances that often give rise to terrorist campaigns?

While Gupta and Moghadam examine the roots of terrorism in general terms, Jack Levin and Arie Perliger's books each have a specific geographic focus. Levin's *Domestic Terrorism* brings the story close to home by describing domestic terrorist activity in the United States over the last half century. Perliger's book, *Middle Eastern Terrorism*, offers an account of terrorist activity in the region of the world with which such violence is most closely identified.

Finally, we believe that young readers will come away from this series of books with a much clearer understanding of what terrorism is and what those individuals and groups who carry out terrorist attacks are like. ■

CHAPTER 1

DEFINING TERRORISM

In August and September 1983, there was a marked increase in violent clashes between Islamic terror activists and U.S. Marines in the southern parts of Beirut, the capital of Lebanon. Beirut had become a focus of U.S. military activities, to the displeasure of the city's residents, and terrorist activities increased as a result. The American military units were part of an international peacekeeping force that had been stationed in Lebanon in 1982, in an effort to resolve the political crisis there. The situation in Lebanon had worsened in 1975, at the outbreak of the Lebanese civil war, and again in 1982, with the Israeli invasion of southern Lebanon. More specifically, the United Nations' decision to send foreign troops to Lebanon reflected the apprehension in the international community regarding the crisis in this part of the Middle East. It was feared that the Israeli incursion into southern Lebanon and the resulting flight of Palestinian terror organizations to Beirut would lead to unprecedented bloodshed.[1]

In Lebanon, leaders of the Shiite minority (a Muslim group consisting of devotees of Ali, the fourth successor of the Prophet Muhammad) who were affiliated with Hezbollah, vowed that "Allah would take revenge on America for its actions in Lebanon." Indeed, revenge was not late in coming. On October 23, a suicide bomber blew up a truck laden with explosives at the Beirut airport, near the entrance to the U.S. Marine barracks. The massive explosion caused the building to collapse, and within minutes, 241 U.S. Marines were killed. The impact of the blast was so overwhelming that many survivors were incapable of reconstructing the moments just before the explosion. One survivor said, "All I can remember is that the terrorist was smiling." Local security services and the Americans forces went on a manhunt, seeking out those responsible for the attack. Evidence led them directly to the Shiite Hezbollah organization and, indirectly, to two countries that took part in the operation—Syria and Iran—both of which sympathized with Hezbollah and provided it with financial and ideological support.[2]

This suicide operation was the most serious terror attack against the United States or its allies until, of course, the September 11, 2001, attacks. Aside from its unprecedented intensity and unparalleled number of casualties, though, the event proved to the world that terrorism was still a viable weapon to be exploited by ethnic, national, and religious groups to attain political goals. In the next 21 years, this assertion was validated by the more than 6,000 globally-occurring terrorist attacks.[3] Among the most prominent of these events were the September 11 attacks on the United States; the bombing of Pan Am Flight 103 over Lockerbie, Scotland, in December 1988; the sarin gas attack in the Tokyo subway launched by the

Aum Shinrikyo cult in 1995; the detonation of a truck loaded with explosives near a government building in Oklahoma City; and the upsurge of suicide terrorism in cities all over Israel in the 1990s and early 2000s.

Terrorism, a phenomenon with different faces, can be approached from many perspectives. First, it serves a variety of ideologies. There are organizations that commit terror in their attempts to fulfill national goals (they wish to attain political sovereignty for the group they claim to represent), and there are groups for whom terror comes from their religious beliefs and a desire to force those religious principles on people in a certain area. A great deal of terrorism in the twentieth century was also committed by radical left-wing groups supporting communist or Marxist ideologies, such as the RAF (Red Army Faction) and RZ (Revolutionär Zelles), groups of youths in

Shiites

Shiite Muslims belong to the Shia, which in Arabic means "a faction or a sect." In the early days of Islam, the term was used to describe those Muslims who asserted that Ali ibn Abi Taleb, the cousin of Muhammad, the prophet of Islam, was Muhammad's rightful successor, both as ruler and as religious leader. The Shiites believe that Muslim sovereignty was passed down by God's commandment to the family of the prophet. Therefore, they believe, the imams (religious leaders) were the successors of the prophet, and the last imam will appear "at the end of time," bringing justice to the world.

Because of the history of conflict between the Shiites and the Sunni (the dominant Islamic group), about the identity of the successor of the prophet, the Shiites still perceive themselves as a deprived and persecuted minority in Islam. They are found mostly in Iran, Iraq, southern Lebanon, Bahrain, and Kuwait, and represent about 10 percent of Muslims worldwide. The worldwide Muslim population is approximately 1.2 billion.

Germany in the 1960s, who demanded that the Social-Democratic Political Party in West Germany return to Marxism in its original form.[4] In yet other cases, terrorism has been employed by extreme right-wing organizations supporting various fascist ways of thinking. These include the AN (National Alliance) in Italy.[5] Terrorism has been used by many groups over wide geographic areas, against diverse targets.

Despite this pervasiveness, in the last 40 years, one specific area of the world has become especially identified with terrorism: the Middle East. This has happened for a number of reasons. First, terrorism has become a dominant and widespread tool for attaining political goals and social change in the Middle East. Second, in contrast to the terrorism that evolved in Europe and Latin America, Middle Eastern terrorism has not restricted itself solely to the geographical area where it originated but has also been exported to other regions in the world. A case in point is the great number of Palestinian terrorist attacks against Israel in the 1970s that were carried out in the international arena, such as the notorious 1972 Munich Olympics attack against Israeli athletes (in which 11 competitors were killed). Today, although its logistic center remains in the Middle East, Islamic terrorism is directed at targets not only in the Middle East but also in Europe and North America. In addition, in comparison to other global terror organizations, Middle Eastern terrorist groups have made more extensive use of lethal tactics and novel methods. Suicide terrorism, for example, has its roots in the Middle East, and its implementation is particularly prominent in that region.

Any attempt to understand contemporary terrorism in depth requires a basic knowledge of terrorism in the Middle East. This book examines the evolution of terrorism and the ways it has been used in the Middle East and neighboring countries. Our study begins with the first appearance of terrorism in the region after the end of World War II and ends with the present. The first third of the book addresses the definition of terrorism, as well as the features of terrorism and the principal ways it is used. The second third deals with the development of terrorism in the Middle East from World War II to the early 1980s. The book's final third discusses the developments and manifestations of Middle Eastern terrorism during the last two decades of the twentieth century and the beginning of the new millennium. In addition, we will try to draw some conclusions from our account of terror in the Middle East and to predict the future of Middle Eastern terrorism, based on its intense and multifaceted history.

DEFINITIONS AND PRINCIPAL FEATURES

Terrorism has played a critical role on both the national and international stages for many years, but it is one of the most difficult social phenomena to define. Security agencies, statesmen and politicians, the media, and even laypeople have tried to answer the question, "What is terrorism?"

Definitions have come from various groups, according to their aims and characteristics. It comes as no surprise, then, that many are likely to quote the expression, "A terrorist in the eyes of one person may be regarded as a freedom fighter by another."

Why is terrorism so difficult to define? First, the concept of terrorism has many facets. This is especially evident in three central respects: terrorism's goals, its operational methods, and its targets. Terrorism has been employed in the pursuit of a wide range of goals, such as addressing religious, territorial, and class struggles. Over the years, terrorists have employed a variety of operational tactics: bargaining attacks (where terror is used as a bargaining chip), taking hostages, hijacking airplanes, suicide attacks, assassinations, incitement, and threats. In recent years, some terrorist organizations have in fact resorted to unconventional types of weapons of mass destruction. During different periods, varying targets have been attacked in order to advance political goals. For example, the nationalist liberation organizations in the 1950s mainly struck at military targets, whereas the leftist organizations of the 1970s struck capitalist and political targets. On the other hand, religious organizations active in the last few decades have operated primarily against civilian targets in their efforts to produce mass casualties.

A second difficulty in defining terrorism is that "the truth is in the eye of the beholder." Members of different religions and nationalities in different geographic areas will use the term *terrorism* according to their own political beliefs. For example, although in the eyes of the West and "the free world," the leader of the al Qaeda organization, Osama bin Laden, is considered an archterrorist, he is regarded by many Muslims as a kind of Robin Hood, someone who fights the wealthy rulers who steal oil riches from Arab countries. According to this view, common Arabs are deprived, and therefore, bin Laden's objective is to achieve justice for all class members, even if that means causing harm to civilians of the rich countries. At the same time, although many Israelis consider Palestinian suicide attacks to be murderous acts of terror, there are those in the Western world who view Palestinian organizations and their members as freedom fighters struggling to end the oppression of their people.

This problem of defining terrorism is also noticeable among the very same agencies that fight terrorism (often called counterterrorism). These organizations describe terrorism according to their own objectives, and it is occasionally possible to see how different agencies in the same country might have different definitions for the term *terrorism*. For instance, the FBI's definition states that terrorism is "the unlawful use of force or violence against persons or property to intimidate or coerce a Government, the civilian population, or any segment thereof, in furtherance of political or social objectives."[6] The CIA defines the same term as the "threat of using or the actual use of violence for political goals by individuals or groups on behalf of a ruling government or against it."[7] The first definition stresses the operational aspect of terrorism; the second emphasizes its subversive or revolutionary character.

A third reason terrorism is difficult to define is that it is dynamic. Its operational methods and targets are continuously changing, and therefore, defining it becomes complex. As a result, the meaning of the term *terrorism* has changed over time. With the advent of the new millennium, terrorism as a method of struggle was also adopted by independent groups who fought in the name of religion, the quality of the environment, and other issues.[8]

Although academic literature on the phenomenon of terrorism also defines terrorism in various ways, most definitions have a number of elements in common: They consider

The Sunni

The Sunni make up the majority of the Muslim world, 90 percent of more than a billion Muslims. The Sunni live according to the Sunna, a concept that in Arabic means "custom" or "way of life," which existed in the tribal society of the Arab Peninsula even before the days of Islam. During this early period, the Sunna was considered the admirable and appropriate behavior of the tribal elders. From the rise of Islam, the Sunna became the way of life of the Prophet Muhammad, and it is believed every Muslim should emulate him. Sunni Islam is divided into four schools of law: the Hanafi, the Maliki, the Shafi'i, and the Hanbali, which is the strictist of the four. The Hanafi is the most moderate. The four schools do not differ in religious principles.

In the seventh century, because of differences of opinion regarding the successor to the Prophet Muhammad, a group split off from the Sunni. This group has been known as the Shia (Shiites). In general, Sunni society is more moderate than the Shiite, but even among Sunnis, there are extremist groups who aspire to set up a theocracy in the Muslim world, according to the model that existed at the time of the Prophet Muhammad.

terrorism to be "intentional use of, or threat to use violence against civilians or against civilian targets, in order to attain political aims."[9]

In the following chapters, we will explore theories about terrorism, then analyze the emergence of terrorism in the Middle East during the 1950s and its development over the years. Special attention will be devoted to certain countries during different time periods.

CHAPTER 2

FIRST SEEDS OF ISLAMIC TERRORISM:
EGYPT AND SYRIA

Egypt is one of the major players in the Arab and Muslim world, and some claim it is, in fact, the most significant. Two crucial sociopolitical processes took place in Egypt at the beginning of the twentieth century that greatly affected its progress as a nation. The first was the awakening of local patriotism among the Egyptian leadership. Following World War II, this patriotic spirit was manifested in the aspiration to unify the whole Arab world under Egyptian dominance, an inclination otherwise known as Pan-Arabism or Nasserism. This policy gained momentum especially with the formal ascent to power of Gamal Abdel Nasser, who became leader of the Egyptian government in 1954.[10]

The second key process was the response to the demotion of religion from a position of influence in Egyptian politics and society. At the end of the 1920s, two prevailing schools of thought in Egypt began to work toward the renewal and empowerment of the Islamic heritage in the country. The first was led by spiritual leaders and academics. The second school of thought was the establishment of the Muslim Brotherhood movement by Hassan al-Banna in 1928. This movement aimed to bring people back to Islam by educational and humanitarian means.[11] Within a short time, however, this movement also resorted to the use of terrorism.

The goal of the Muslim Brotherhood, according to al-Banna, was to transform Egypt into a country under the rule of Islamic religious law (Sharia), while subordinating education, the economy, and other state apparatuses to the spirit of Islam. Along with al-Banna, Sayyid al-Qutb (1906–1966) became one of the Muslim Brotherhood's main ideological leaders. Al-Qutb, the founding father of jihad in Egypt (the word *jihad* originally meant "effort" in a religious context; however, with the onset of the Islamic wars, it has taken on the meaning of a violent holy war), wrote many ideological manifestos that were used as a platform for similar organizations in the Arab and Muslim world. In his most famous book, *Maalem Fi Altrik* ("Milestones"), al-Qutb concluded that countries that are not Muslim were ignorant and heretical and that Islam was the only true religion. The only way for Islam to rule the world is by means of jihad.[12]

Over time, while making appeals to Egyptian citizens to return to Islam, the Muslim Brotherhood was engaged in activity on another level—the effort to liberate the country from British rule. The movement concentrated particularly on attempts to eliminate Egyptian and British officials. Their most prominent assassinations were the January 1945 killing of Amin Ottman Peha, an Egyptian statesman who had close connections with the British government, and the

The Muslim Brotherhood continues to be the most popular opposition group in Egypt. This photo shows a 2005 Muslim Brotherhood demonstration in Cairo, during which participants demanded greater freedom to form political parties. In that year's elections, the Brotherhood won 88 parliamentary seats—20 percent of the total.

December 1948 slaying of Mahmud Fahmi Nokrashi, the Egyptian prime minister.[13]

The escalation of violence on the part of the Muslim Brotherhood prompted the Egyptian administration to adopt an iron-fisted approach and take action to dismantle the movement. After the assassination of Nokrashi, the movement was declared illegal, and in February 1949, the movement suffered another severe blow when al-Banna was killed by agents in the service of the Egyptian government.[14]

As Nasser rose to power in the early 1950s, the movement was allowed to resume its activities. In the first months of Nasser's rule, good relations in fact existed between the Egyptian government and the movement. Nasser envisioned Egypt becoming a modern, progressive, and secular state, though, which sharply contrasted with the worldview of the Muslim Brotherhood. The Brotherhood wanted to renew the Islamic legacy and its laws and not succumb to Western political perceptions, which they felt Nasser had adopted. Once again, the two sides were drawn into confrontation. These clashes peaked with the attempt by a Brotherhood activist on Nasser's life during a speech he gave on October 26, 1954, in the city of Alexandria. The failed assassin, Mahmoud Abd al-Latif, together with five other activists, was caught and sentenced to death. As a consequence, the movement was again banned, more than 4,000 of its members were detained, and a number of its leaders and central figures were executed by hanging.[15]

The Officers' Coup in Egypt

On July 23, 1952, the Egyptian army carried out a coup, overthrowing the monarchy of King Farouk, and Egypt became a republic. The military act was only a precursor to basic changes in Egypt. In three years, not only was the monarchy abolished, but the upper-class landholders lost their status and were replaced by the army and the civil service. In addition, by 1955, the army had signed an agreement with Great Britain, and the last British soldiers left Egypt, which now had full independence. The Egyptian coup of 1952 was the first radical revolution in the Arabic-speaking countries of the Middle East. It became a model for similar revolutions that were to occur a few years later in other states in the region.

The government takeover was initiated by a group of young army officers, including Gamal Abdel Nasser and Anwar Sadat, both of whom subsequently served as presidents of Egypt. These officers were members of the Free Officers Movement, established in 1949. After the coup, the movement set up the Revolutionary Command Council under the leadership of Muhammad Naguib, although real power remained in the hands of Nasser, who continued to lead the movement until he died in 1970.

In the 1950s, Egypt not only suffered from domestic terrorism, but was also an exporter of terrorism. A prime example was the Palestinian *Fedayeen* (in Arabic, "one who sacrifices himself"). These forces were essentially squads of infiltrators who operated along the temporary border between Israel and Egypt (the Gaza Strip). Individuals or groups stealthily crossed into Israel to steal, sabotage, and kill, and the Fedayeen maintained a state of constant military tension along armistice borders, with the aim of weakening the emergent state of Israel.[16] One of the deadliest Fedayeen operations was the massacre at Ma'ale Akrabim. A bus carrying civilians from Eilat to Tel Aviv was ambushed by Fedayeen militants. Eleven passengers were killed.

In addition to staging deadly ambushes, the Fedayeen also planted explosives. On November 2, 1954, they set off bombs in the houses of an Israeli *moshav* (a co-operative Israeli settlement), Patish, in the Negev, and attacked Jewish agricultural settlements in the south. In January 1955, farmers of the moshav Beit Hashlosha were attacked while tilling their fields.[17] One was killed, and others were injured.

In 1955, the Egyptians granted formal patronage to these activities and recruited Fedayeen squads from among the Palestinian population in the Gaza Strip. The goals of the squads were principally to gather intelligence and to maintain the state of tension along the border. In March 1956, the Fedayeen regiment, consisting of some 600 fighters, was established. It mainly carried out gunfire attacks against Israeli forces and conducted a number of raids into Israeli settlements. The regiment was destroyed in 1957.

In the early 1960s, the Egyptian government began once again to focus primarily on domestic religious terrorism. In light of the movement's assassination attempts on Egyptian political figures, President Nasser declared war on the Muslim Brotherhood. Egyptian security forces launched a comprehensive campaign of arrests of the movement's activists and executed prominent and important leaders. The highest ranking leader was Sayyid al-Qutb, who was put to death in 1966. Once the Muslim Brotherhood's leadership was eliminated, the movement was significantly weakened.[18] Radical Muslim unrest in Egypt did not subside, however, so new, alternative organizations using terrorist methods began to appear.

Among other fundamentalist groups of note active in Egypt were Al-Takfir Wal-Hijra; W'Al-Hijra; Shabab Mohammed (Mohammed Youth); Al Jihad (holy war or effort); and the Islamic Liberation Party, the Egyptian faction of what was originally a Palestinian movement. All these organizations were involved in conspiring to commit murders, bearing arms, distributing pamphlets with the aim of overthrowing the government, and stirring up the Egyptian public. The resulting agitation led to the violent mass riots of 1981–1985, especially in the cities of Assiut and Ismailia.[19]

Toward the end of the 1970s, an organization called the Islamic Group (Al Jamaat Al Islamiyya) also appeared in Egypt. Initially, this group was set up under the patronage of the Egyptian government following the death of Nasser, who had believed that it would help him fight left-wing groups that had sprung up in the student sector. Quickly, though, it became a violent and obstinate opposition to the regime and today is considered the most powerful terrorist organization in Egypt.[20]

The groups just reviewed collectively perpetrated more than 700 acts of terror during the 1970s and early 1980s. These attacks used a variety of methods. In their efforts to carry out terrorist operations and sabotage in Egypt, some of these organizations, such as Al-Takfir, collaborated with other groups hostile to the Egyptian government, such as the Libyan government.[21] Perhaps the most infamous incident committed with Libyan assistance was the hijacking of Boeing Flight 737 in August 1976 by Egyptian terrorists who were also radical Muslims. A short while after it took off from Cairo, the plane was forced to land in the Egyptian city of Luxor. Hijackers then demanded the release of Libyan, Palestinian, Yemenite, and Egyptian prisoners from Egyptian prisons in exchange for the lives of the passengers taken hostage on board the plane. In the end, Egyptian commando forces succeeded in overpowering the hijackers and were able to rescue all of the passengers.[22]

Toward the end of the 1970s, the various Islamic organizations set their sights on President Anwar Sadat, who had replaced Nasser after his death in 1970. Sadat was targeted because he had taken steps to reconcile with Israel. Although the efforts of the Mohammed Youth organization to carry out a violent coup and the kidnapping of President Sadat in April 1974 failed, the group succeeded in assassinating him on October 6, 1981. This was an important achievement for Islamic terror in Egypt.

SYRIA

Much like in Egypt, the political violence and terrorism in Syria was mainly a result of radical Islamic movements. The first Islamic organization to be established in Syria was the Muslim Brotherhood, in 1944. The Brotherhood was a direct consequence of the Muslim charity movements that had already been functioning in Syria for two decades, and, more important, it was an offshoot of the "mother movement" in Egypt. According to the Muslim Brotherhood, Syria should become a centralized, powerful, industrialized, and modern country, but, at the same time, it should reject the secularism of Western society and embrace the spirit of Islam.[23]

Mustafa al-Siba'i, the leader of the Brotherhood until 1957, claimed that the movement was not a tangible, concrete body, such as a political party or association, but rather a spiritual power related to the very existence of Muslim society. In 1963, the Brotherhood was declared illegal because of its opposition to the Syrian government and also because of the public appeals of Brotherhood members to rebel against the government and

Accompanied by his vice president, Hosni Mubarak, President Anwar Sadat (center) salutes military personnel at a parade on October 6, 1981. Moments later, Sadat was assassinated by Muslim extremists hidden in some of the parade's military trucks.

replace it with an Islamic regime. The northern faction of the movement persisted in its violent resistance to the Syrian government, however, and in 1964, it engaged in a violent uprising against Syrian rule in the northern city of Hama, which was suppressed with a very firm hand.[24] After the battle, dozens of corpses littered the city streets. In 1965, only one year later, the riots resumed under the initiative of the Muslim Brotherhood, and this time, the riots spread to the capital, Damascus.[25] Despite the movement's success in being able to stir up violent resistance to the Syrian government, its activities in the 1960s were only a taste of the terrorism Syria would see in later years.

In November 1970, following a military takeover, Hafez al-Assad took control of the Syrian government. Al-Assad was able to establish a stable, centralized government mainly because of the well-developed and widely branched network of his political party, the Ba'ath (revival) Party, which succeeded in gaining a hold among large sectors of Syrian society. However, the Sunni-Muslim majority in Syria viewed al-Assad and his people, who were of Alawi origin, as their social and cultural inferiors, who had suddenly been transformed from the servants into the masters of Syria.[26]

Despite splintering in 1963 into different factions, the Syrian chapter of the Muslim Brotherhood continued its struggle against the secular government of the Ba'ath Party. With the intention of reducing the tension between the movement and the government, al-Assad made an effort in the early 1970s to reconcile the various Islamic factions in order to bring them closer to his government. In 1972, he embarked on a pilgrimage to Mecca and obtained the approval of Lebanon's Shiite imam to assure all Shiites that the Alawis were, for all intents and purposes, Muslim Shiites and not infidels. In 1973, al-Assad even agreed to the Brotherhood's demand that the Syrian president must be a Muslim.[27]

These efforts failed, and three years later, in response to Syria's invasion of Lebanon, the Muslim Brotherhood spearheaded an organized terror campaign against the Syrian government in an attempt to topple it by force. Syrian government officials were killed during the rebellion, and several government institutions and installations (mostly in northern

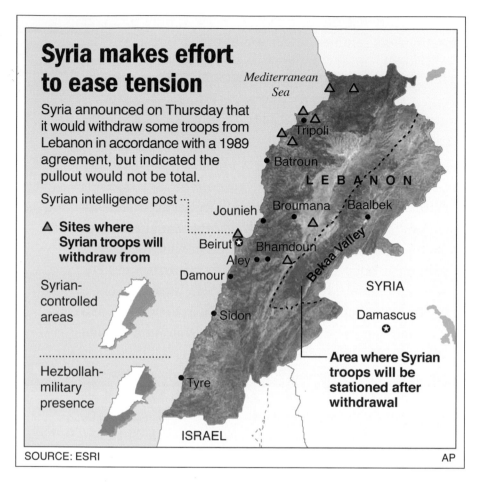

Syria makes effort to ease tension

Syria announced on Thursday that it would withdraw some troops from Lebanon in accordance with a 1989 agreement, but indicated the pullout would not be total.

⋯ Syrian intelligence post

△ Sites where Syrian troops will withdraw from

Syrian-controlled areas

⋯ Hezbollah-military presence

Mediterranean Sea

Tripoli
Batroun
LEBANON
Jounieh   Broumana   Baalbek
Beirut   Bhamdoun
Aley
Damour
Bekaa Valley
SYRIA
Sidon
Damascus

Area where Syrian troops will be stationed after withdrawal

Tyre

ISRAEL

SOURCE: ESRI   AP

Figure 2.1 **This graphic illustrates the plan for the withdrawal of Syrian military troops from Lebanon. Originally embedded in 1976 to keep peace during Lebanon's civil war, Syria continued its military and political presence until 2005, when it finally bowed to international pressure and evacuated all troops.**

Syria) were attacked. In 1979, particularly under the influence of the Islamic revolution in Iran, the riots worsened and Brotherhood activists attacked Ba'ath Party headquarters in the northern cities of Halab, Hama, Homs, and Idlib. In the same year, one of the most severe attacks took place against the Syrian army when Islamic terrorists killed 83 Alawi cadets of the Syrian Artillery Academy.

In the early 1980s, resistance to the Syrian regime continued to grow, and on June 25, 1980, there was even an attempt on al-Assad's life. This incident intensified the overall level of confrontation between the Syrian regime and Islamic activists, and, in 1982, al-Assad issued an order to the Syrian army to put an end to the Islamic radical uprising at any cost. The price proved to be very high. In Hama (the northern city that was the hotbed of Islamic organizational activity) alone, it was reported that nearly 25,000 people were killed as the Syrian army brutally cracked down on Islamic activists, even making use of chemical weapons. In 1982, Islamic terrorism was effectively eliminated for good in Syria. Ironically, the government of Syria subsequently began using terrorism for its own political needs in the Middle Eastern arena.

CHAPTER 3

PALESTINIAN TERRORISM:
THE NATIONAL SECULAR PHASE

The Palestinians originated from an Arab-Bedouin population that settled in an area called "Israel" by the Jews and "Palestine" by the Arabs during the Islamic conquests of the Middle Ages. The Arabs in the area of Palestine raised sheep, grew forage and pasture crops, and developed an extensive agricultural infrastructure. In 1834, the Arabs rebelled against the leader of the Egyptian lands of the Ottoman Empire, Damat Ibrahim Pasha. From that time forward, the Palestinian people have been fighting for a state of their own in Palestine, and during each period, they have been up against a different ruler, whether it be the Turks, the British, or Israel.[28]

In the wake of the military confrontation between Israel and the Arab countries over the establishment of the state of Israel

(1947–1949), the Palestinian people were dispersed throughout the Middle East. This resulted in the establishment of Palestinian refugee camps in Jordan, Gaza, Syria, and Lebanon. Further geographical-political changes brought on by the Six-Day War in June 1967 (such as the Israeli takeover of East Jerusalem, the West Bank of the Jordan River, the Gaza Strip, and the Golan Heights), uprooted even more Palestinians and forced them to take up residence elsewhere. They settled in different areas, such as Kuwait and other countries near the Persian Gulf.

In the first few years after the establishment of Israel, many Palestinians and their leaders believed that the solution to their plight would come from the Arab countries. They assumed that the state of Israel was only a temporary situation and that in a short while they would be able to return to their homes in Israel. During the course of the 1950s, though, as it became apparent that Israel was gradually turning into a regional military power and that the state was gaining broad support in the international community, the Palestinians began to realize that their political situation as a group of refugees dispersed all over the Middle East was not necessarily temporary.[29]

In addition, many Palestinians felt it was important to take action and make sure the Arab public was continuously aware of the Palestinian problem in order to further an Arab resolution. These processes, as well as the emergence of violent liberation organizations in the developing world after World War II, led to the establishment of the Fatah movement in Cairo, Egypt, in 1957, and its institutionalization as an organization in 1959. *FATAH* is the acronym in Arabic—in reverse letter order—for the "Palestinian Liberation Movement"; in Arabic, the word also means "conquest" or "victory."[30]

This Palestinian movement was headed by Yasser Arafat, a civil engineer from Al-Azhar University in Cairo. Fatah believed that Israel must be fought with force and by armed struggle so that the Palestinians could reclaim their political right to establish a sovereign state on Palestinian lands. Fatah was the first to coin the term *armed struggle against Israel,* a struggle with an aim that was not to defeat Israel militarily but rather to cause harm to its citizens and perhaps even pave the way for a military confrontation between the Arab armies and Israel.

Fatah was not the only group that demanded a Palestinian armed struggle. In January 1964, sponsored by Egypt, the PLO (Palestine Liberation Organization) was established under the leadership of Ahmad Shukeiri. This organization immediately became a rival of Fatah, particularly because of its success in setting up its own operational-combative wing: the Palestinian Liberation Army. However, the rivalry between the two

The Gaza Strip

The Gaza Strip is an area on the southern coast of Israel, inhabited until recently by 1,400,000 Palestinians and 8,000 Jews. Until 1967, Gaza was under Egyptian authority, although Egypt never claimed sovereignty over the area. In 1956, during the Sinai Campaign, the Gaza Strip was captured by the Israeli Army but was returned to Egypt after the war, along with the rest of Sinai. In 1967, following the Six-Day War, Israel took control of Gaza, and it remained under Israeli control until the Palestinian Authority was established according to the Oslo Accords, signed by the Israelis and the Palestinians in 1993. According to the Oslo Accords, civilian and military control in the major cities, Gaza, Rafiah, Khan Yunis, and Dir el-Balakh would be Palestinian, whereas Israel would continue to control the Jewish settlements in Gaza and its main transportation arteries. At the end of 2004, the Israeli parliament accepted a plan proposed by Prime Minister Ariel Sharon to evacuate all civilians and military forces from Gaza, an act that was carried out in 2005. Today, the area has become a focal point for widespread Palestinian terrorist activity, especially on the part of Hamas. This includes suicide attacks, explosives, and missile fire at Jewish settlements in Gaza and other areas of Israel.

organizations did not last for long because, in the years 1966–1969, Fatah gradually took control of the PLO by electing its own people to the organization's leadership.[31] Eventually, the PLO became an umbrella organization that politically and organizationally oversaw all the other Palestinian terrorist organizations. As a result, since 1974, the Arab countries have recognized the PLO as the sole and lawful leading authority of the Palestinian nation.[32]

Fatah was the most central, familiar, and dominant of the many Palestinian organizations of the time. According to the definitions set forth by the PLO, its activities were not terror but rather comprised a legitimate battle for the rights of an oppressed people.[33] "The meaning of armed struggle," as put forward by the Fatah movement's leader Haled al-Hasan, "is not to defeat the Israeli Defense Forces but rather to provoke Israel, to sow the seeds of fear among its citizens and, at the same time, to kindle the spirit of resistance and struggle in the Arab world."[34]

Starting in the mid 1960s, Palestinian terrorist groups carried out many different types of terrorist actions. These attacks grew more persistent after the Six-Day War between Israel and the surrounding Arab states. Among these were the repeated attempts of terrorist groups to damage the water and transportation infrastructures in Israel. On December 31, 1964, Palestinian terrorists tried to sabotage the main water carrier in Israel. Although the terrorist squads were captured by both the Israeli army and the Egyptians as they tried to cross the border from Egypt into Israel, their efforts gained widespread publicity in the Arab world and were a source of considerable concern among the Israeli public. Other prominent acts of sabotage on Israeli infrastructures by Palestinian terrorist organizations were the March 1967 explosion of the water tanks in Arad, a city in southern Israel, and the blast that immobilized the Tel Aviv–Jerusalem railway in October 1966.

The operation that could have caused the worst disaster at that time, however, was attempted on June 24, 1969, when a

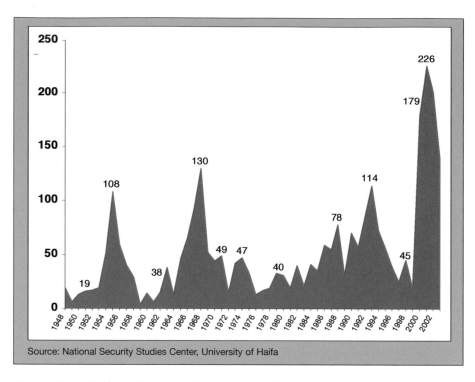

Source: National Security Studies Center, University of Haifa

Figure 3.1 **This graph shows the number of Palestinian terrorist attacks in Israel, per year. Note that after a leveling off in the 1970s and a sharp decline in 1999, attacks spiked to nearly ten times that amount in 2001.**

main pipeline of refined oil in the Haifa Bay was rigged with explosives. The Haifa Bay area in general is a center of industrial factories and oil refineries—and sabotage could cause a huge disaster. The blast that resulted led to a substantial fire along the entire pipeline system, and it took firefighters five hours to put it out. Most of the damage was financial, as about 1,000 tons of fuel were burned. There were no injuries.[35]

Palestinian terrorist acts were not limited to the country's infrastructure; they were also aimed at clearly identifiable civilian sites. The PLO's intention was to spread fear and hysteria among the Israeli population. One of their most notorious operations was the explosion of a car bomb on Agrippas Street in Jerusalem on Friday, November 22, 1968. In the early hours of the morning, two members of Fatah parked a car laden with explosives on Agrippas Street near an important commercial area of the city. Two hours later, the car exploded, killing 12 people and injuring dozens more.[36]

Coinciding with their operations inside Israel, at the beginning of 1968, Palestinian terrorists also waged an intense campaign on the Israeli–Jordanian border. They conducted hundreds of infiltrations and terror attacks on Israeli border settlements and fired several types of long-range weapons, such as Soviet Katyusha rockets and heavy mortars, from stationary positions or mobile vehicles. The use of this kind of weaponry allowed terrorists to bombard Israeli targets without directly confronting the Israeli army and, in this way, to extend the range of their terrorist activities.[37]

During those years, the Jordanians allowed Palestinian organizations to use their country as a base for operations against Israel. Fatah took advantage of this opportunity and established a training base and an organized and efficient military in Jordan. Along with military operations, there were also political activities, which included the functioning of the organization's Central Committee in the capacity of an executive body and the establishment of a Revolutionary Council in order to act as a type of parliament.

In March 1968, one of the more severe attacks perpetrated by Palestinian terrorists at that time took place on the Jordanian border. A busload of Israeli schoolchildren traveling down the Arava Road (which connects the northern part of Israel to the southernmost point and runs along the Jordanian border) activated mines planted by Palestinian terrorists and burst into flames. As a result, one child and the doctor accompanying the school trip were killed, and another 28 were injured. In the wake of this incident, the Israeli government felt that there was a genuine need to put an end to Palestinian terrorism, so it launched a series of military operations against Palestinian terrorist bases in Jordan.

The most prominent of the Israeli operations, known as the Karameh Operation, was carried out on March 21, 1968. Although the Israeli army was able to kill 60 Jordanian fighters and more than 120 Palestinian terrorists in this operation, the fact that the Karameh fort itself was not captured and that 28 Israeli soldiers were also killed was a shot in the arm for the Palestinians and a demoralizing blow for the Israelis.

PALESTINIAN TERRORISM IN LEBANON

In September 1970 (what is now known as Black September), Jordanian forces drove most Palestinian terror activists out of Jordan, and more than 3,000 Palestinians were killed.[38] Consequently, Palestinian terrorist organizations had to relocate their activities to Lebanon. Despite their need to rebuild a military and organizational infrastructure in Lebanon, the 1970s were the heyday for Fatah and other Palestinian organizations. They conducted numerous and diverse attacks against Israeli targets—both military and civilian—and created such a broad network of social services in the south of Lebanon that the area was called "Fatahland." Here, the Palestinians set up courts of law, imposed taxes, provided military training for Palestinian youths, and, most of all, inspired pride and raised the hopes of the residents of this region.[39]

Fatah was very active and committed a variety of attacks against Israel. On November 6, 1970, organization activists were able to smuggle two explosive charges into the Tel Aviv central bus station, killing 2 and wounding 34.[40] In July 1971, Fatah members launched Katyusha rockets at a hospital and school near the city of Petah-Tikva, killing 2 and injuring 20. In the same month, Katyushas aimed at Tel Aviv by Fatah members from their hiding place in Judea and Samaria caused the deaths of 4 people and wounded 30.[41] On March 5, 1975, Fatah set out on one of their bolder acts of terror. A detail of Fatah militants took control of the Hotel Savoy in Tel Aviv and held hostages. In exchange for their release, they demanded

Egyptian mediators try their hand

Egyptian mediators met with Palestinian factions in Gaza on Monday to try to persuade them to lay down their arms and give the peace plan a chance. At the same time, mediators were seeking guarantees from Washington that Israel would stop targeting Hamas leaders.

Palestinian terror groups represented in cease-fire talks

Group	Hamas (Islamic Resistance Movement)	The Palestine Islamic Jihad (PIJ)	Al-Aqsa Martyrs' Brigades (Fatah's military wing)
Origin	Formed in late 1987 as an outgrowth of the Palestinian branch of the Muslim Brotherhood	Originated among militant Palestinians in the Gaza Strip during the 1970s	Formed right after the current Palestinian intifadah began in September 2000
Position	Committed to establishing an Islamic Palestinian state in place of Israel	Committed to the creation of an Islamic Palestinian state and the destruction of Israel	Aims to drive Israeli military and settlers from West Bank, Gaza and Jerusalem
Activity	Uses political and violent means, including terrorism and large-scale suicide bombings; strength is concentrated in Gaza Strip and West Bank	Conducted large-scale suicide bombings against Israeli civilian and military targets; in 2001, it targeted Israeli interests	Carried out shootings and suicide operations against Israeli military and civilians; first group to send a female suicide bomber
Funding	Some funding from Iran; relies mostly on donations from Palestinian expatriates around the world.	Receives financial assistance from Iran, limited logistic assistance from Syria	Unknown

SOURCE: U.S. State Department "Patterns of Global Terrorism 2002"   AP

Figure 3.2 This graphic profiles three Palestinian terror groups represented in cease-fire talks with Egyptian mediators in 2003.

that the French consul be handed over to them and that a plane be put at their disposal so they could return to Lebanon. The incident ended when an Israeli commando force stormed the hotel and regained control; however, they were unable to prevent the deaths of 11 Israelis, who were killed in the process.[42] Toward the end of the 1970s, Fatah decided to abandon terrorism on an international scale and concentrate solely on terrorist attacks inside Israeli territory. This change in tactics was adopted particularly in an effort to build up international support for its activities.

In addition to Fatah, which, beginning in the 1970s, was the main Palestinian faction of the PLO, various other Palestinian organizations set out from Lebanon on operations against Israel, as well as targets associated with Israel throughout the world. The more significant of these organizations are the Popular Front for the Liberation of Palestine (PFLP); the Democratic Front for the Liberation of Palestine (DFLP); the Popular Front for the Liberation of Palestine–General Command; Fatah: The Revolutionary Council; Black September; Arab Liberation Front; Palestinian Liberation Front; and the Abu Musa faction.

CHAPTER 4

TERRORISM IN PURSUIT OF NATIONAL LIBERATION

At the beginning of the eighteenth century, Algeria, which formerly had been part of Morocco and Tunisia (today, all three countries exist independently), became an independent colony of the Ottoman Empire. In 1830, French forces occupied Algeria, and for the next 130 years, Algeria remained a French colony. French settlers brought with them their education, language, and customs; eventually, their culture became central to the daily life of Algerian residents. At the same time, there was considerable neglect of the Arabic language and the Islamic heritage that had been part of the country's history since the introduction of Islam to North Africa in the seventh and eighth centuries.[43]

THE FLN IN ALGERIA

In the early 1950s, other resistance movements in the Arab world began to influence the Muslim people in Algeria, and they moved to bring French rule to an end. The dominant force in this struggle was the FLN (National Liberation Front), which spearheaded the struggle from 1954 until 1962, the year in which Algeria gained its independence.[44] The FLN took its cue from various groups in Algerian Arab society who, as far back as the 1930s, had used terrorism to preserve the Muslim identity of the country.

The notion of urban terrorism was adopted by the FLN with the help of Frantz Fanon, a French doctor and thinker who remained in Algeria during the FLN's anticolonialist struggle against the French army. Fanon, who became one of the most prominent ideological leaders of the FLN, believed that only violent struggle could lead to the end of colonialism in modern times. In his view, only the heavy costs that foreign governments would have to pay facing urban terrorism could truly persuade them to leave the colonies.[45] In order to achieve this goal, Fanon believed that terrorism should be aimed at the urban middle class and that harming and terrorizing this class would create anarchy, which would eventually lead to its flight. The abandonment of the cities by the middle class—upon which the colonial regime was structured—would ultimately bring about the defeat of the conquerors in the struggle against colonialism.

Members of the FLN applied Fanon's teachings; they carried out attacks on institutions and representatives of the French regime and mounted a massive assault on the civilian population of French settlers. In the first stage, the FLN concentrated mainly on French military posts in the city of Algiers. They also launched raids on French settlers in major cities and on farmland owners in the country. At the beginning of April 1955, in addition to attacking Europeans in Algeria, the organization also began to terrorize Muslim residents. The reason for this was twofold: to force their Algerian "brothers" to volunteer themselves (and the provision of material supplies) to the organization and to deter Muslim Algerian citizens from collaborating with the French establishment.[46]

By the middle of 1956, as FLN operations gradually escalated, and particularly after the killing of 123 civilians, including women and children, in the town of Phillipeville, the French army decided to step up its counteroffensive measures. Thousands of soldiers stormed the center of Algiers, carried out mass arrests, and executed two members of the FLN by guillotine. In the summer of 1957, members of the FLN set off a bomb in a casino in Algiers, causing many deaths and a great deal of damage.[47] About the same time, the FLN gradually began to gain control over areas in the mountainous southern part of Algeria. It imposed military rule, set up training bases, collected taxes, and recruited activists to its ranks. By 1957, it is estimated that members of the FLN were responsible for the deaths of more than 7,000 civilians and soldiers.

On September 30, 1957, the FLN increased the intensity of its attacks and launched what was to become known as the Battle of Algiers. First, three organization operatives planted and detonated explosive devices in three locations in Algiers, including the city's Air France branch office. Then, the FLN continued to attack, committing more than 800 acts of terror per month throughout the spring of 1958. In response, France deployed 400,000 additional soldiers in Algiers, but this did not stop the FLN. The group maintained its heavy schedule of terrorism, and eventually the high costs of keeping the colony outweighed what the French government could afford. Finally, in 1962, the president of France, Charles De Gaulle, conceded defeat and granted independence to Algeria.

The new Algerian government maintains ties to other Arab terrorist groups. Since the ascent of the new government in Algiers in 1962, mutually close and empathic relations have been forged between the Arafat-led Fatah organization and the Algerians. In 1965, two years after Fatah opened its offices

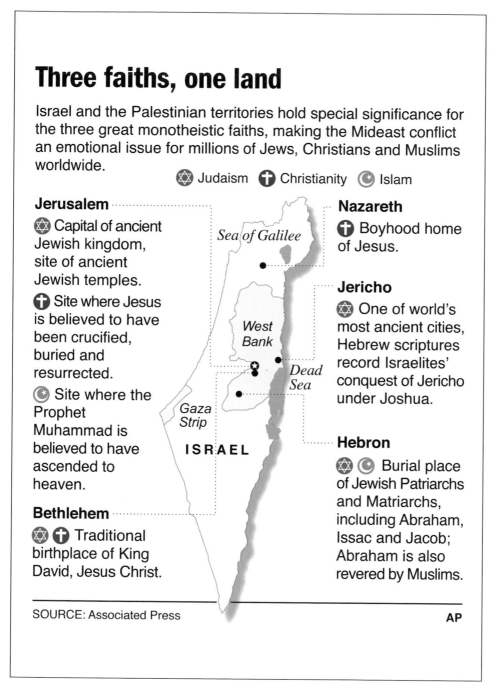

Three faiths, one land

Israel and the Palestinian territories hold special significance for the three great monotheistic faiths, making the Mideast conflict an emotional issue for millions of Jews, Christians and Muslims worldwide.

✡ Judaism   ✝ Christianity   ☾ Islam

Jerusalem
✡ Capital of ancient Jewish kingdom, site of ancient Jewish temples.

✝ Site where Jesus is believed to have been crucified, buried and resurrected.

☾ Site where the Prophet Muhammad is believed to have ascended to heaven.

Bethlehem
✡ ✝ Traditional birthplace of King David, Jesus Christ.

Sea of Galilee

West Bank

Dead Sea

Gaza Strip

ISRAEL

Nazareth
✝ Boyhood home of Jesus.

Jericho
✡ One of world's most ancient cities, Hebrew scriptures record Israelites' conquest of Jericho under Joshua.

Hebron
✡ ☾ Burial place of Jewish Patriarchs and Matriarchs, including Abraham, Issac and Jacob; Abraham is also revered by Muslims.

SOURCE: Associated Press

AP

Figure 4.1 The significance of holy sites in Israel and Palestinian territories to the religions of Judaism, Christianity, and Islam are presented in this graphic.

in Algiers, the country's ruler, Houari Boumedienne, agreed to train Fatah forces in his country.[48]

JEWISH TERRORISM IN ISRAEL

The first Jewish terrorist groups in Israel were formed in the 1930s and 1940s as part of the Jewish community's struggle to achieve political independence and political sovereignty in

The Zionist Movement

The Zionist movement originated in the 1880s and called for a return of the Jewish nation to the land of Israel, where it would create its own state. The movement was intended to make this aspiration a reality. It resulted, in part, from the feelings of Jews in the Western world that, despite the processes of modernization and democratization that these nations were undergoing, Jews were still suffering from discrimination and sometimes from persecution. In 1882, during a period known as the First Aliya (First Wave of Immigration), the first Zionist Jews began to immigrate to Israel. By 1936, an additional four waves of immigration had brought the number of Jews living in Israel to more than a half million.

The dominant leader of the Zionist movement during its early history was Theodore Herzl. He is still considered the "prophet" of the state-to-be. The Zionist movement encouraged Jews to immigrate to Israel and was involved in building and developing the land. New settlements were established, an educational system was created, a culture developed, and land purchased. The group achieved its goal on November 29, 1948, when the State of Israel was established by a decision by the United Nations. The land was divided into two states, one Arab and one Jewish. On May 14, 1948, David Ben-Gurion, the first prime minister of the State of Israel, officially declared its independence. The Zionist movement subsequently carried on its activity in the framework of the Jewish Agency and the Zionist Organization, and continued to bring Jews to Israel, while collecting contributions for Israel from Jews all over the world.

Israel. The British controlled Israel at that time, and although British foreign minister Lord Balfour had assured the leaders of the Zionist movement (which believed in the immigration of Jews to the Land of Israel and the establishment of a Jewish state) that Britain was committed to the idea of establishing a national home for the Jews, their policy during this period, in practice, was far from an actual implementation of this promise. The Jews were especially angry at the quotas imposed by the British regarding the number of Jews who were allowed to immigrate to Israel, the restrictions on the purchase of lands by Jews, and the preferred status granted to the Arab population (who, demographically, were the majority). Two of the foremost Jewish organizations founded before the establishment of the State of Israel and that fought for the end of British control over Israel were the National Military Organization (the Etzel, or the Irgun) and the Fighters for the Freedom of Israel (the Lehi).

ETZEL

From 1919 to 1948, to defend Jewish settlements from Arab attacks, leaders of the Zionist movement in Israel founded an active, essentially military organization called the Haganah. Similar to other voluntary defense organizations, the Haganah was primarily involved in defensive operations, including providing security to isolated Jewish settlements. Its operational and military capabilities were very limited. In the summer of 1929, however, Jewish neighborhoods were attacked by Arabs in the four mixed (Jewish and Arab) cities of Jerusalem, Tsfat, Tiberius, and Hebron, resulting in more than 130 fatalities. In wake of these incidents, it was decided to upgrade the Haganah's activities and turn it into a military organization with enhanced capabilities and nationwide deployment.[49]

These changes did not satisfy all the members of the organization, particularly those who belonged to the Jerusalem chapter. They demanded that the organization develop its

New members of the Haganah march as part of their training in this 1948 photo. The Haganah was the foundation of Israel's modern army.

offensive capabilities significantly and go out and attack Arab targets. Moreover, this Jerusalem branch was adopted by the right-wing political leader of the Zionist movement, Ze'ev Jabotinsky. Before long, the group split off from the Haganah, became the military arm of the Revisionist movement (a faction of the Zionist movement that followed the European right wing of the time), and came to be called "Etzel." The Haganah became in practice the military arm of the Mapai (the movement that controlled the Zionist movement and held more socialist views).

In the years following the separation, the Etzel devoted its time to organizing and establishing itself as an organization, especially in preparation for illegal operations, bringing Jews to Israel by sea with boats it had acquired. In 1936, however, the Great Arab Revolt broke out. Arab bands engaged in hostilities and violence against the British and the Jewish community in Israel in response to what they regarded as an attempt to deprive them of their right to rule the region.

The Arab Revolt provided Etzel with an opportunity to set itself apart from the Haganah: It chose not to follow the Haganah's "policy of restraint" toward the Arab population. Instead, the Etzel leaders decided upon a terrorist approach, carrying out arbitrary attacks on the Arab population. On April 20, 1936, Etzel members killed two Palestinian workers in a banana plantation, and two days later, they threw a grenade at Arab passersby in Tel Aviv and Jerusalem. In August 1936, Etzel terrorists shot at a passenger train. The Etzel's terror campaign against the Arab population lasted until the end of the Arab Revolt in 1939 and included more than 60 attacks.[50] During this period, the group used four major tactics: assassination attempts, attacks on transportation routes, shootings, and the use of explosive devices.

Encouraged by its success and the experience built up by its members, the Etzel expanded its range of activities to include ambushes and systematic attacks on major transportation arteries, which included shooting at a bus carrying Arab passengers in July 1938,[51] attacking another bus with explosives in September 1937,[52] and shooting at a truck driven by an Arab in November 1937. The group also carried out shooting attacks on Arab population centers. The organization's new strategies also included the detonation of explosives by remote control. The most dramatic act in this regard was the planting of a mine in the Arab market in Haifa in July 1938, an attack that resulted in the deaths of more than 70 Arabs.

With the outbreak of World War II, the Etzel decided at first to declare a cease-fire in its struggle against the British authorities. In February 1944, however, at the initiative of its leader at the time, Menachem Begin, the Etzel ended the cease-fire.

Several things prompted this decision; prominent among them were signs of the allied forces' approaching victory. The most infamous terrorist act of the new campaign against the British was the 1946 bombing of the King David Hotel in Jerusalem, which housed the central government offices of the British Mandate. Eighty-two people were killed in the attack, including civilians, and dozens more were injured or registered as missing. After the establishment of the State of Israel, the group was dismantled.

LEHI

The ceasefire declared by Etzel in 1939 after World War II had broken out led to the withdrawal of a group of the organization's members, under the leadership of Yair Stern, to form the Lehi. More than any other Jewish organization, the Lehi viewed acts of terrorism as legitimate tools in the realization of the vision of the Jewish nation and a necessary condition for national liberation.[53]

After years of missteps, disbandment, reorganization, and ineffective actions, for the first time in the history of the organization, the Lehi group was successful in gaining public sympathy for their efforts and organization. This followed the assassination of Lord Moyne in Egypt in November 1944. Lord Moyne, who had held the position of the minister of the British colonies since the beginning of World War II had been appointed on January 28, 1944, to resident minister of the Middle East. Moyne had long been marked as hostile to Jewish settlement because of his long-standing support for the establishment of an Arab federation in the Middle East and in light of his anti-Semitic speeches (for example, a speech in which he had called for the need to grant sovereignty to Arabs in Israel because the Arab race was purer than the mixed Jewish race). In November 1944, two members of the Lehi shot and killed Lord Moyne in Cairo and, as a consequence, were executed.[54]

In the first weeks after the establishment of the State of Israel, the Lehi managed to perform one more act of terror that triggered a wide-ranging counteroffensive of the Israeli security forces against the organization. On September 16, 1948, Lehi militants killed the Swedish diplomat Count Folke Bernadotte, who had arrived in Israel as a United Nations mediator. It would appear that the Lehi's basic mistrust of the Israeli interim government led to the assassination. Attempts at achieving a cease-fire between the fledgling State of Israel and the surrounding Arab countries, and all mediation efforts, were regarded by the Lehi as a negative development. They saw these steps as the beginning of a dangerous process in which the various powers were liable to return and regain control of the region in order to restore political stability and to reduce the lands of the Jewish State. Consequent to the assassination, the entire leadership of the Lehi organization was imprisoned, and the group was finally dissolved.

After the establishment of the State of Israel, in the early 1950s, two other Jewish terrorist organizations emerged. The first was a small group of ex-Lehi members called the Kingdom of Israel, which chiefly targeted diplomatic representatives from countries of the Communist Bloc in Israel. Their actions stemmed from the desire to protest the rise of anti-Semitism in Eastern Europe at the time. Therefore, their operatives planted bombs in the Czech and Russian consulates, and they tried to assassinate the chancellor of Germany, Konrad Adenauer, with letter bombs. The second organization was called the Covenant of the Zealots and consisted of young religious Jews who took it upon themselves to establish religious rule in Israel according to the dictates of the Halakha (Jewish law).

They principally attacked commercial institutions in Israel that did not uphold Jewish law and its directives, such as keeping kosher or refraining from traveling or using electricity on the Sabbath. Activists of both organizations were captured within a few months after the initiation of their activities and, in effect, were never able to develop a substantial organizational infrastructure. After the disbanding of these two organizations, Jewish terrorism disappeared from the Israeli scene for a period of 25 years, until the beginning of the 1980s, when Messianic Jewish groups whose programs also included violence and terror emerged.

CHAPTER 5

TERRORISM IN IRAN AND AFGHANISTAN:
THE SEEDS OF THE GLOBAL JIHAD

Iran, a major country of the Middle East, lies on the seam between the Middle East and the continent of Asia. The Persian Empire was a distinguished power during the greater part of the history of the Middle East. During the nineteenth century, though, it had to fight for its independence against foreign Western powers vying for control of the natural resources of the Persian Gulf. One essential phase in Iran's (then, still called Persia) process of achieving modern statehood took place between 1921 and 1926 when Reza Khan established the Pahlavi dynasty and in 1926 was crowned shah, the ruler of the state. In those years, the Persian shah embraced two important policies. First, he waged a persistent war on the northern and southern borders of the country against regions and tribes that opposed the government—a war that until the end of the 1920s was successful. Second, he ousted the Ulamaa (the Shiite wise clerics) from positions of power throughout the country. By putting the educational system, courts, and other social networks under state control, he reduced the influence of Islam on Persian society. In its relations with the West, the shah's administration did not hesitate to refer to the "sinister religious fanaticism" of the populace.[55]

This relationship between the shah and the Shiite clerics and their supporters, the mujahideen, had its ups and downs over the years, but relations deteriorated following the reforms the shah attempted to implement in the health system, education, economy, and social life of Iran. These reforms, intended to create a modern, Western civilian infrastructure in Persia, suffered a fatal blow during World War II, when the much-needed supply of civilian and military commodities was blocked and income from oil exports subsequently decreased. The invasion of Persia by Soviet and British forces during the war did not do much to improve the shah's standing.[56]

The shah's persistence against the religious establishment after World War II led to the emergence of terrorist organizations that wanted to reinstate Islamic tradition as the center of social and political life in the country. The two most prominent of these groups were the Mujahideen Khalq, formed in 1965, and the Fedayeen, established in 1963. The Mujahideen Khalq was initiated by a group of Tehran University graduates who sought to integrate Islamic Shia and Marxist doctrine, and to institutionalize an Islamic-socialist republic in Iran.[57] Moreover, organization activists regarded violent struggle as a pivotal tool in the realization of their vision, and therefore, in almost every one of their political manifestos, they stressed that "armed struggle is an historical necessity."[58]

The Fedayeen organization was created by students from low socioeconomic backgrounds, who were easy to recruit because they had very little to lose. These students sought to return Islamic religion and tradition to the place they enjoyed formerly in Persian politics and society. Beginning in 1963, the organization mounted sporadic attacks against public property and killed public figures. Only in 1971, though, after a period of several years, during which the two organizations concentrated on developing solid institutional infrastructures, did these groups begin to engage in more intensive action against the shah's government. At the same time, they were prepared to pool resources with other organizations in South America and Algeria, as well as with the PLO. Their collaboration with the PLO was particularly close, and members of both movements even fought side by side in Jordan during the events of Black September and trained together in Fatah camps in Lebanon.[59]

Members of the Fedayeen were active in the Gilan Forests in northern Iran, where they initiated, among other operations, an attack on the headquarters of the Iranian army on February 8, 1971, which led to a response that included the detention and elimination of many activists. The government's offensive did not halt the campaign of terror, however; the Mujahideen Khalq continued to rob banks throughout the country and attempted to murder Western visitors, though mostly targeting the American military and civilians. The following are examples of a number of prominent attacks by these organizations.

On May 30, 1972, a bomb was set off at the information office of the United States Embassy in Tehran, killing one American and wounded two others. The next day, a car bomb prepared by the Mujahideen Khalq exploded adjacent to the U.S. Air Force Base in Tehran, but this time there were no casualties. On June 9, 1970, members of the Mujahideen Khalq planted a bomb near the counters of the Israeli airline, El Al, and in January 1973, the Fedayeen placed a bomb in the offices of Pan Am airlines in Tehran. In both cases, there were no casualties. In May 1975, three members of the Fedayeen killed two U.S. Air Force officers. The terrorists were captured and eventually executed. Additional attacks were made on police stations, the Reza Shah Mausoleum in Tehran, and also on the offices of the British Petroleum Oil Company.[60]

Beginning in October 1978, the Mujahideen Khalq and Fedayeen intensified their struggle, launching a string of attacks on various institutions of the shah's regime and political figures associated with him. The fight was defined by the groups as "open and extensive" in order to show the Iranian people that the shah's regime was, in fact, vulnerable and could be defeated.[61] The organizations' targets were both external (symbols and representatives of the capitalist-liberal-democratic West) and domestic (the shah's pro-Western regime). The escalation in violence and disorganization in the government provided fertile ground for the outbreak of the Islamic revolution in Iran in 1979. This revolution heralded far-reaching changes in

Jihad

The word *jihad* comes from the Arabic root *jhd,* meaning "to make an effort to do something." In Islam, the word became identified with a holy war to convert non-Muslim populations and territories. Current usage originated in the military organization created by the Prophet Muhammad at the dawn of Islam. Muhammad first invoked jihad to fight opponents in the city of Mecca and afterward against the inhabitants of territories conquered by Islam in the Arab Peninsula and elsewhere.

Jihad, considered a religious law, has been a principal instrument in the struggle against non-Muslims. A Muslim killed during a jihad is believed to have ensured his place in paradise. It should be emphasized that a jihad may be carried out nonviolently, when populations are willing to accept the authority of Islam, to live under its rule, and to be defended by it, paying a "head tax" to the Muslim ruler. From the mid-twentieth century, the term *jihad* has been used increasingly by extreme Muslims both against Arab secular governments and against Western states. For example, Osama bin Laden declared jihad against Jews and Christians in 1998.

Mujahideen march in Kabul's Independence Day parade in 2003. After the fall of the Mohammad Najibullah regime in 1992, the mujahideen held power without forming a united government until they were ousted by the Taliban in 1996. In 2001, regrouped as the Afghan Northern Alliance, they forced out the Taliban with assistance from U.S. forces and formed a new government under Hamid Karzai.

the use of terrorism, not only *in* the country itself but also terrorism initiated *by* the country, an issue that will be discussed in Chapter 7.

AFGHANISTAN

Afghanistan lies in the eastern part of the Middle East, forming a kind of "wedge" between that region and Asia. The country borders Pakistan to the south and Iran to the west, and its northern parts are bounded by countries from the former Soviet Union. Muslim fundamentalism had already evolved in Afghanistan in the late 1960s, as schools for the study of Islam became more established. At these institutes, Islamic law was taught and cells of the Muslim Brotherhood developed,[62] although they were still characterized by social-political, nonviolent action. Even so, the empowerment of religious institutions in Afghanistan indeed provoked unease in the Afghan government.[63]

At the end of the 1970s, the Soviet Union also began to publicly express its concern over the increasing volatility of the Afghan regime in light of the increasing strength of radical Islamic elements in Afghan politics and society. The Soviets feared that Islamic zeal in Afghanistan would "trickle down" into the Muslim regions in the south of the Soviet Empire and endanger the Soviets' hold on these countries, which are also abundant in natural resources. Realizing that the current instability might lead to the downfall of the Afghan regime, which it supported and which might possibly be replaced by a hostile Islamic regime,[64] on December 28, 1979, the Soviet Union invaded Afghanistan.

The Soviet Union's initial foray led to a war that lasted more than ten years, waged between Muslim fighters and the Soviet Red Army and its allies in the country. The Muslim forces that fought the Soviets consisted of an assortment of groups, such as the Islamic Movement in Afghanistan, the Islamic Party, the Islamic Alliance of Afghan Mujahideen, and the Islamic Revolutionary Party. Together, they were called the Mujahideen (i.e., participants in an Islamic holy war) and the majority comprised Islamic activists from Iran and Pakistan who made the journey to Afghanistan in order to help in the struggle against the Soviets and the anti-Muslim regime.[65]

In upcoming sections of the book, we will discuss how the war in Afghanistan led to the establishment of the organizational infrastructure otherwise known as the Global Jihad. This included a broad consortium of Islamic organizations, most of them active in the Middle East and of which the most notorious was al Qaeda.

A NEW KIND OF TERRORISM

The end of the 1970s also marked the conclusion of the first stage in the evolution of terrorism in the Middle East. From the beginning of the early 1980s, global terrorism, as well as terrorism in the Middle East, underwent a number of changes in ideology, operations, and organization.

In a broad sense, two principal incentives prompted different groups in the Middle East to opt for terrorism as a method for fomenting change. The first was the nationalist, anticolonial motivation. In this case, terrorism was applied against external rule by an organization that functioned as a representative of a certain ethnic group and whose ultimate purpose was to create a new political entity or, alternatively, bring about the withdrawal of a foreign ruler. The main examples, and the ones that have so far been the focus of this book, were the terror actions of the FLN in Algiers against the French government, the Jewish terrorist organizations in Israel against the British rulers, and the Palestinian struggle with Israel.

The second incentive for the use of terrorism stemmed from religious motives, or the wish to institute regimes in the spirit of Islam in various countries. This type of terrorism was usually applied against the local government, whether the country had already gained independence or whether it was in stages of negotiation with the colonial administration. Prominent examples include Egypt, where the Muslim Brotherhood actively functioned against the independent regime to the point that the heads of this movement were either imprisoned or executed, and Syria, where an additional chapter of the Brotherhood operated.

Although anticolonial terrorism was, to a certain degree, productive, as in the case of Jewish terrorism in Israel and in the Algerian case (in both instances, acts of terrorism contributed to the withdrawal of foreign forces and the institution of independent states[66]), the success of fundamentalist Islamic terrorism was limited until the end of the 1970s. In effect, in most of the countries of the Middle East, Islamic movements were suppressed and their political clout curbed. Violent Islamic struggle began to bear fruit only toward the end of the 1970s and at the beginning of the 1980s, with the success of the Islamic revolution in Iran and the empowerment of violent Islamic factions in Afghanistan.

As for the geographic dispersal of terrorism in the Middle East, until the beginning of the 1970s, terrorism was mostly restricted to areas within the borders of the countries where it flourished. This is quite unlike present-day terrorism, which may cross borders and oceans and, in many cases, does not restrict itself to a single political region. In fact, terrorism in the Middle East, up until the early 1970s, was characterized by being local in nature.

Nonetheless, nationalist as well as religious ideological notions certainly did cross from one country to another and provided inspiration to local organizations. In such a manner, chapters of the Muslim Brotherhood in Syria, Egypt, and Iran acted against local rulers in the effort to realize common ideologies. Ideas circulated among neighboring countries, and, in many instances, organizations collaborated strategically, even though they may have belonged to different ideological frameworks. For example, Iranian Islamic organizations took advantage of Fatah training bases in Lebanon in order to train and prepare their fighters. In the early 1970s, Middle Eastern terrorism was exported to other regions. Principally responsible for this phenomenon were the Palestinian organizations; they perpetrated acts of terrorism on planes, in airports, and within a variety of noninvolved countries, such as the murder of the Israeli athletes at the 1972 Munich Olympics.

Another central process that began to gather momentum mainly toward the end of the 1960s was the transformation of Palestinian terrorism into the most dominant violent activity in the Middle East. To a great extent, Palestinian terrorism overshadowed all other terrorist organizations active in the

Middle East at the time and also provided inspiration for a succession of national liberation organizations all over the world. This inspiration derived from the fact that the methods of action developed by Palestinian groups proved to be a genuine upgrade in the ability of terrorist organizations to achieve broad exposure—on a worldwide level—for their political aims. At the same time, Palestinian terrorism caused serious damage to targeted Israeli and international civilian infrastructures and was successful in creating a sense of anxiety, fear and hysteria amid broad sectors of the public.

The next chapters will describe the further development of terrorism in the Middle East, the next stage of which began in the 1980s.

CHAPTER 6

THE START OF THE NEW MIDDLE EASTERN TERRORISM

In the 1960s and 1970s, terror had become a central factor in Middle Eastern politics. In the 1980s and 1990s, however, several political processes that took place both internationally and in the Middle East caused many to assume that terrorism in the Middle East was on the decline. These included the end of the Cold War, the defeat of Iraq in the Persian Gulf War in 1991, and the signing of the Oslo Peace Accords between Palestinian representatives and the government of Israel in 1993.

Within a brief period of time, however, this assumption was proven wrong. Despite the signing of the Oslo Accords, Palestinian terrorist organizations persisted in their struggle against Israel, and despite the conquest of Iraq by the United States and its allies, there has in fact been a sharp escalation in terrorism in recent years in this region. Furthermore, the al Qaeda organization, which surfaced and laid its foundations in Afghanistan, shocked the world with one of the worst terror aggressions of all time— the September 11, 2001, attacks on the U.S. World Trade Center and Pentagon buildings. Since then, al Qaeda has continued to initiate acts of terrorism in the Middle East and elsewhere. At the same time, albeit on a much smaller scale, Jewish acts of terrorism have also become more prominent in Israel.

Consequently, researchers have increasingly argued that terrorism in the Middle East is changing its nature. These changes apply to the way terrorists operate, how they are organized, and what they think. Operationally, there has been an increase in the use of tactics that attempt to transform terror into a more lethal weapon. For example, "force multipliers," such as suicide bombers, have become more common, and there has also been a greater emphasis on civilian targets, increasing the potential for mass casualty disasters. Whereas terror groups in the 1960s and 1970s struck at targets mostly to gain widespread media exposure, Middle Eastern terrorists today focus mainly on high-density (crowded) targets that cause greater harm to a larger number of civilians. In ideological terms, the dominance of religious fundamentalist groups has grown at the expense of left-wing and nationalist terror groups. In conflicts that used to be essentially about having one's own country, such as that between the Palestinians and the Israelis, there has been a greater penetration of religious elements. In terms of organizational makeup, more and more terror groups have abandoned the hierarchy typical of traditional armies that distinguished organizations in the 1960s and 1970s, and instead developed networks of cells that are capable of carrying out terror attacks more autonomously and in different geographical areas. This new structure has enhanced the organizations' ability to survive and has also made it possible to improve contact among organization leadership, activists, and supporters. To a great extent, terrorist groups in the Middle East have adopted new methods, making it possible to maximize the effectiveness of their actions in the dynamic Middle Eastern theater.

TERRORISM IN EGYPT AT THE END OF THE TWENTIETH CENTURY

The 1981 assassination of Egyptian president Anwar Sadat may have marked the peak of a wave of terror that targeted the Egyptian government following the signing of peace agreements with Israel in 1979, but Sadat's death did not bring about any real change in Egyptian policy toward Israel. Nor was there any significant change in the terrorism aimed at the Egyptian regime. Sadat was succeeded by his vice president, Hosni Mubarak, who declared he would uphold the policy of his predecessor toward Israel.

In consequence, Islamic opposition organizations, such as the Islamic Jihad, the Islamic Liberation Organization, and the Islamic Group, continued to wage their campaign of terror. Between 1981 and 1986, there were no fewer than 700 terror events; these included assassinations of administration figures, planting bombs in various central urban locations (such as the bomb at the Cairo Hilton in May 1988), violent clashes with Egyptian security forces in the cities of Assiut and Ismailia, and attacks on foreign forces in Egypt (for example, the shooting at an American gunship in the Suez Canal in May 1986).[67] Because they also set their sights on undermining the conciliation process between Israel and Egypt, however, Egyptian organizations also attacked Israelis in Egypt. For example, in June 1984, a band of radical Egyptian activists laid in wait for an Israeli diplomat in the suburbs of Cairo, and when they identified his car, they fired at him, wounding him in the shoulder. A year later, in August 1985, Egyptian terrorists killed an Israeli diplomat from the Israeli embassy in Egypt and wounded his wife as they were driving in the area of the embassy.[68]

Despite the violent actions of Islamic organizations, Mubarak, in comparison to his predecessors, assumed a more

soft-line approach to their activities. For example, during the
first decade of his government, President Mubarak allowed
Islamic organizations to establish independent forms of media
(mostly their own newspapers) and also gave his permission
for their representatives to run and be elected to the Egyptian
Parliament in the 1984 and 1987 elections. Mubarak believed
that providing Islamic organizations with alternative (primarily
political) channels of action would perhaps curb their motivation to continue to resort to violence. At the same time, though,
this freedom provided Islamic organizations with the opportunity to establish themselves, organize, and strengthen their
influence on Egyptian society. No longer was one speaking of
isolated political movements operating underground.

In his struggle with the Islamic organizations, Mubarak set
up three main objectives of his policy of restraint. First, he
would try to do his best to suspend terror attacks perpetrated
by Islamic movements in Egypt. Second, he would try to prevent
Islamic fundamentalists from getting a hold of key positions in
institutions of law and education, academia, and the Egyptian
parliament.[69] This second objective was especially significant
in view of the virtual takeover of most of the major professional
unions in the country by members of the Muslim Brotherhood,
such as the Lawyers Union in September 1992, as well as
impressive wins by the Brotherhood in municipal council
elections in November of that same year.[70] The third challenge
was to limit the return of and clamp down on the activities of
Egyptian terror activists who came back from the war in
Afghanistan and began to initiate terrorism both against Egyptian authorities and on an international scale.[71]

The success of Mubarak's policy of restraint was limited,
however, and during the 1990s, Islamic terrorism in Egypt once
again reared its head. The direct threat of terror on the stability
of the government in Egypt placed the struggle against Muslim
insurgency very high if not foremost on the Egyptian administration's agenda.[72]

What features of terrorism made it an acute problem for Egypt once more—and a threat to the stability of the Egyptian government? One type of terror targeted members of the Coptic (Christian) community in Upper (southern) Egypt, particularly because members of this sect were regarded as opponents of Islam by the radical Islamic opposition in Egypt. These actions included violent clashes with security forces that defended the community and vandalism of churches in the Alexandria vicinity and suburbs of Cairo.

Another type of terror was aimed at intellectuals who objected to Islamic fundamentalism in Egypt. Perhaps the two most prominent examples of this hostility were the assassination

The Copts

Many scholars believe the Copts, or Native Egyptian Christians, to be most directly descended from the ancient inhabitants of the country. The name *Copt* is a distortion of the word *Egypt,* which was used by the Greeks to identify the country's inhabitants. According to historical records, the Copt church, founded by Mark the Evangelist, was well established in Egypt by the third century. The head of the Copt church, the patriarch, lives in Cairo.

After the Muslim occupation of Egypt in the seventh century, many Copts converted to Islam. Those who did not became a persecuted minority, at first by the Arab Muslims and then by the Ottoman Turks. Beginning in the nineteenth century, the Copts' status in Egypt gradually improved, and church members were accepted into the government and military. In 1963, the sect received permission to set up a Coptic Council to deal with issues of marriage, education, and property ownership in the community. At the beginning of the twentieth century, the status of the Copts improved even more when a member of the church, Boutros Ghali, served as Egyptian prime minister, until he was assassinated in 1910. Today, Egypt's 4.5 million Copts make up 6 percent of the country's population.

Nobel Prize–winning novelist Naguib Mahfouz is shown posing in the Gamaliya quarter of Cairo, where he grew up. Ever since his 1994 assassination attempt by Muslim extremists, Mahfouz has lived under constant bodyguard protection.

of Faraj Fuda, a journalist and well-known critic of radical Islam in Egypt, in June 1992,[73] and the attempted assassination of Naguib Mahfouz, winner of the 1988 Nobel Prize in literature, in October 1994.[74] Mahfouz was accused by Muslim radicals of writing in a style that was too permissive, realist, and liberal, to the point of "blasphemy."

In October 1992, Islamic terrorists in Egypt also began to take aim at the tourist industry, one of the mainstays of the

Egyptian economy and a primary source of foreign revenue. The most severe of all aggressions ever to be perpetrated on Egyptian territory against foreigners took place in the city of Luxor in November 1997. Militants from the Al Jamaat Al Islamiyya organization, using guns and hand grenades, assaulted a large group of tourists, killing 58 foreign citizens and 4 Egyptians.[75]

These events caused critical damage to the Egyptian tourist economy and led to a 40 percent decrease in tourism to Egypt that year. Further, these events were highly detrimental to the development of the tourist industry during that period—an industry that received an investment of 60 percent of the overall outlay of the Egyptian government in 1992. In April 1996, the "deadly decree" for tourists in the country was extended to Cairo itself when 17 Greek pilgrims were murdered at the Europa Hotel in Cairo.[76]

In response to the criticism leveled at terrorists, members of the Jamaat and the Jihad declared that the reason for their assault on tourism was twofold. First, these attacks undermined the very foundations and stability of the government. Second, they also led to a lessening of the "evil influence" that Western tourists brought with them to Egypt.[77]

Despite their aggressive actions against the tourism industry, the Islamic organizations did not give up their attempts to bring about political change by means of eliminating high-ranking officials of the Egyptian administration. For instance, in June 1995, radical Islamists in Egypt tried to take the life of President Hosni Mubarak while he was visiting the Ethiopian capital Addis Ababa. In the wake of this grave incident, the Egyptian government heightened its efforts to rein in the terror that was on the loose in Egypt. Security forces tried to drive the rampant terror toward the southern border of the country, as far as possible from the major cities.[78] In response to the resumption of the Egyptian government's iron-fisted policy (according to some estimates, more than 29,000 extremist

Muslims are currently in Egyptian prisons, accused of endangering the government),[79] Islamic organizations once again chose to boycott government elections.

Another consequence of the government's approach toward terrorist organizations was that Egyptian organizations began to "export" terrorist attacks to Western countries. One such incident was the explosion at the Egyptian Embassy in Pakistan in November 1995, when a truck laden with about 550 pounds (250 kilograms) of explosives blew up at the entrance to the facility. As a result, 17 people were killed and 60 were injured. This attack was also executed by Al Jamaat Al Islamiyya.[80]

Egyptian terrorist cells today consider themselves as part of a broader network of Islamic organizations whose long arms reach all over the world. They collaborate with their equals in other Muslim countries and take part in attacks that are initiated by activists who are not Egyptian. For example, Egyptian terrorists were directly involved in detonating the massive car bombs in Nairobi and Dar es Salaam in August 1998, at the American embassies in Kenya and Tanzania.[81] In the September 11 attacks, one of the commanders of the operation—Mohammed Atta— was Egyptian. He was a passenger on American Airlines Flight 11, the plane that crashed into the northern tower of the World Trade Center. Further, prominent officers of Egyptian fundamentalist organizations Al Jamaat Al Islamiyya and Al Jihad Al Masri, such as Ayman al-Zawahiri, Ahmed Rifai Taha, and Mustapha Hamza, became active under the umbrella framework of the al Qaeda organization, which also absorbed in its ranks additional Egyptian terrorists, some of whom even took part in the war in Afghanistan.

CHAPTER 7

SPONSORS OF TERRORISM:
SYRIA, IRAN, AND HEZBOLLAH

Between 1980 and 1982, the struggle between extremist Muslim forces and the Syrian government gradually escalated. Terrorists attacked army bases and government and political party facilities and murdered military officers and government officials. The confrontation reached a climax on February 22, 1982, in the northern cities of Homs, Aleppo (Halab), and Hama. In Hama, Muslim terrorists almost gained full control; they attacked public buildings (including the city's Ba'ath Party headquarters), government offices, police stations, and Syrian security force headquarters in the city, and executed hundreds of government officials.[82]

To suppress the uprising, the Syrian army bombarded Hama with cannons, tanks, airplanes, and fighter helicopters, and dispatched

Syrian commandos into the city. Somewhere between hundreds (according to the Syrian government) and 20,000 Islamic activists (according to extremist Islamic forces) were killed; whole parts of the city were completely destroyed.[83] After the events in Hama, Syrian president al-Assad continued to systematically act against extremist Muslim organizations with considerable success, and in 1982, Islamic terrorism in Syria was virtually eliminated.

Although Syria suffered greatly at the hands of violent organizations that opposed its government in the 1970s and 1980s, the Syrian regime was at the same time involved in *exporting* terrorism, particularly by granting patronage to terrorist organizations that served its interests. Syria still promotes terrorism, which in 1996 prompted the United States to declare that country, together with six others, as a state that sponsors and supports terror.[84]

During the 1990s, and despite the peace processes taking place in the Middle East at the same time, Syria continued to be one of the major countries sponsoring terrorism. In fact, the signing of the two peace agreements—the Oslo Accords between Israel and the Palestinians in 1993 and the Jordan-Israeli peace contract in 1994—even further isolated Syria in the Middle East arena, thus compelling it to carry on its support of terrorist organizations as a means of preserving its status in the region. Of particular prominence was Syrian support for the Hezbollah organization, which was engaged in a war of terror and guerrilla warfare against Israel on the Lebanese border, and also its support for Palestinian organizations opposed to the negotiation and reconciliation processes between Israel and the PLO. Even the complete withdrawal of Israel from Lebanon in 1999 (since 1982, Israel had continued to deploy its army along a narrow strip in southern Lebanon) and the changing of governments in Syria did not prevent the Syrians from persisting in their support of various terrorist organizations.[85]

Criticism aimed at Syria as a terror-sponsoring country came not only from the West but also from some of the Arab countries. Principally, Egypt, Saudi Arabia, and Algeria have accused Syria of sheltering terrorists in recent years. In 1996, following the attack on American soldiers in Dharan, Saudi Arabia, the Saudis held Syria accountable for allowing Lebanon-based terrorists unhindered passage through Syria to carry out the attack. As for Egypt and Algeria, both have repeatedly pointed the finger at Syria, which, according to their allegations, has provided refuge for "Afghan Arabs" (that is, veterans of the war against the Soviets) and in this way created a base for them to embark on attacks all over the Arab world. The Syrians, on the other hand, have tried to soften the criticism by extraditing dozens of Muslim officers to various Arab countries in an attempt to reduce the tension between Syria and the rest of the Arab countries.[86]

Further, since the death of Hafez al-Assad in 2000, there has been no discernible, substantive change in Syrian government policy under the rule of his son, Bashar. The Syrian government continues to support Hezbollah, it still encourages and provides aid to Palestinian terror against Israel, and it shows empathy toward and in fact provides assistance to insurgent terrorist groups in Iraq.[87] In this fashion, Syria continues to preserve its status in the international arena as a terror-sponsoring country.

IRAN

After Islamic rule was established in Iran in 1979, the new administration believed that a part of its role was to export the revolution to the rest of the Arab world. With this in mind, the Iranian regime hastened to grant its sponsorship and support to Islamic resistance movements whenever and wherever they sought to supplant a secular government with an Islamic one. In this fashion, Iran provided assistance to Palestinian Muslim organizations in Samaria and Judea in their struggle against the state of Israel. It continued to aid and promote the Hezbollah organization in Lebanon and also helped Islamic resistance organizations that emerged in Algeria, India, Afghanistan, and other places.[88]

However, Iran's support of terror was not limited solely to assisting other organizations—it also made a direct use of terror for its own vested interests. During the last decade of the twentieth century, Iran intensified its involvement in world terror, providing assistance to terror organizations and at the same time dispatching its own terror squads. Among the more prominent organizations that benefited from Iranian backing was Hezbollah. Also benefiting from Iranian assistance was Ahmad Jibril's Popular Front–General Command. Iran was also involved in operations plotted by the Palestinian Hamas and Islamic Jihad.[89]

An example of Iranian terror was the 1991 elimination of former Iranian prime minister Shahpour Bakhtiar, by the Iranian "diplomatic" staff in Paris, which, in effect, was an assassination task force. Bakhtiar was targeted because he was bold enough to mildly criticize the Iranian regime. Other cases include persecution of literary figures connected to the translation and worldwide distribution of Salman Rushdie's book *The Satanic Verses*. For example, its Japanese translator, Norwegian publisher, and Italian translator were all shot at or stabbed under "mysterious" circumstances. All these incidents, as well as the massive assistance provided to terror organizations throughout the Middle East and beyond, earned the Iranians the designation of a "terror-sponsoring state of the first degree" by the U.S. State Department[90] and led to the intensification of American sanctions against Iran.

Iranian involvement has been evident in terror operations conducted in Arab countries with Western leanings.[91] During 1994–1995, Saudi affiliates of Iranian agents executed two large-scale attacks in Saudi Arabia. On November 13, 1995, a booby-trapped car exploded next to a training base of the Saudi Arabia National Guard in Riyadh. In one of the affected structures, three stories collapsed and 7 people were killed, including 5 Americans, and 45 were injured. Saudi Arabian security forces revealed that the perpetrators of the attack were four Saudi citizens sponsored by Iran. A few months later, on June 25, an empty fuel tanker rigged with more than two tons of dynamite exploded at an air force base in Dharan and once again the results were severe—19 dead and about 500 wounded. The investigation after the event led to the conclusion that the terrorists had trained both in Iran and with the Hezbollah organization in Lebanon.[92]

HEZBOLLAH

In the early 1980s, Israel decided to intensify its battle against Palestinian terror organizations and invaded Lebanon. This offensive ultimately led to the emigration of most Palestinian terror organizations from Lebanon. Not long after, however, Israel was forced to deal with a much more determined rival— Hezbollah (Party of God), which became the most prominent terror organization in Lebanon since the 1980s.

Hezbollah's first goal was to rid Lebanon of foreign forces. At the end of 1982, the organization mounted a highly destructive campaign of terror, employing suicide bombers against most of the foreign army forces that resided in Lebanon at the time, also hoping to regain order in a country whose stability was gradually deteriorating—first because of the civil war and then because of the Israeli invasion of Lebanon. Hezbollah's first attacks targeted the U.S. Marine headquarters and the French Multinational Force in Beirut in October 1983. This brought the organization Middle Eastern and international recognition. These two attacks were carried out using a heretofore unfamiliar method— trucks rigged with explosives, driven and activated by suicide bombers.[93]

Not only did Hezbollah engage in the struggle against foreign forces in Lebanon by using suicide bombers, its members were also involved in the systematic kidnappings of Westerners, sometimes resulting in the death of their victims. The most notable of these events was the abduction of the American colonel William Higgins, who was kidnapped and hanged in February 1988.[94]

Hezbollah guerrillas participate in an Al-Quds Day parade in Baalbek, Lebanon, in 2004. Al-Quds Day is an annual reminder of the oppression of Palestine. It is also an occasion for speaking out against Israel and Israel's supporters, such as the United States and Britain.

After the Western military forces pulled out of Lebanon in 1983 and the Israel Defense Forces (IDF) withdrew from Lebanon (to the security zone that it created in the southern part of the country) in 1985, Hezbollah changed its style of operations. First, it almost completely halted its campaign of suicide attacks, which had lost their effectiveness because IDF troops had secured themselves in southern Lebanon in reinforced strongholds. On the other hand, the organization began to wage guerrilla warfare against Israeli forces and unleash artillery fire on settlements in northern Israel. Second, at the same time that it was engaged in these violent actions, Hezbollah began to develop a civilian and humanitarian infra-structure for the Shiite population in southern Lebanon. [95]

Hezbollah's status in Lebanon continued to gain promi-nence during the 1980s and 1990s, particularly after the signing

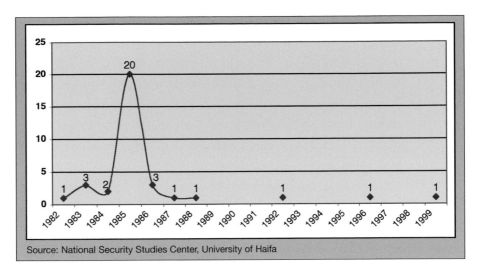

Source: National Security Studies Center, University of Haifa

Figure 7.1 **Hezbollah suicide attacks were at their highest numbers during the 1980s, as shown in this graph, which charts the number of suicide attacks by Hezbollah, per year.**

of the Taif Agreement, which officially decreed the end of the civil war in Lebanon in 1989. In wake of the agreement, Hezbollah remained the only armed political movement in Lebanon and was allowed to be active in two parallel realms. In the military realm, it was able to establish, together with Iranian support and Syrian patronage, training bases, local and regional headquarters, communications networks, and front-line outposts facing IDF camps. In social-political areas, Hezbollah was able to reinforce its status among the Shiite population in southern Lebanon by establishing a broad welfare infrastructure, which included cultural institutions, schools, and charity organizations.[96]

After the leader of Hezbollah, Sheikh Abbas Musawi, was killed by Israel in 1992, Hezbollah stepped up its terror attacks on Israeli targets, including the launching of Katyusha rockets at civilian settlements in northern Israel. The organization performed other infamous operations in the 1990s. In those years, Hezbollah also helped develop the logistic and operational infrastructure for Palestinian suicide terror by providing direct assistance to the Palestinian Hamas and Islamic Jihad. The organization also took pains to stress that these were not terror actions but rather just and legitimate acts of war against the Israeli enemy. Using this justification, Hassan Nasrallah, the current leader of Hezbollah, was quoted as saying "in our world today, talk means nothing, and the world understands only the logic of blood."[97]

Although the organization's violent military actions against Israeli forces in Lebanon decreased after the complete Israeli withdrawal from the country in May 1999, they did continue, albeit in a much reduced fashion. In the wake of the Israeli pullout, Hezbollah now faced the necessity of justifying its continued existence as a military force in Lebanon. Among the more extreme Hezbollah operations after the Israeli retreat was the abduction of three Israeli soldiers to Lebanon, resulting in

The Taif Agreement

The Taif Agreement was signed in the Saudi Arabian city of the same name in October 1989, when the Lebanese parliament declared an official end to the civil war that had ravaged the country since 1975. The agreement, signed under the auspices of Saudi Arabia and, more important, Syria, determined that Lebanese government institutions would be divided equally between Christians and Muslims, and it defined the area of southern Lebanon, an area where the Hezbollah movement was dominant, as an area of complete Lebanese sovereignty. The prime minister of Lebanon at the time, Michel Aoun, a Christian, rejected the accord, maintaining that it enabled the Syrians to continue their patronage over Lebanon and to operate freely throughout the country. Even more serious, the accord, which called for the disarming of all warring factions, left one faction with its weapons: Hezbollah, which continued to rule southern Lebanon even after the agreement and took advantage of its weaponry to attack Israel.

their deaths, on October 7, 2000.[98] In addition, the organization carried on with the occasional antiaircraft gunfire and antitank shelling of Israeli army outposts on the Israeli–Lebanon border.

At the beginning of 2002, the Hezbollah organization stepped up its active support for Palestinian movements warring against Israel; its activists began sponsoring Palestinian acts of terror and in certain cases participated in their plotting and execution.

Despite the organization's "rise to fame," both on the domestic Lebanese scene as well as from a more pan-Arab and Muslim perspective, the United States' appearance as a "resident" in the Middle East, for the time being at least, puts Hezbollah at a kind of crossroads. As far as Hezbollah is concerned, there is cause to persist in the armed struggle, but, on the other hand, its inclusion in the blacklist of world terror organizations casts a shadow on this same position. What is more, its big sponsors, Iran and Syria, are under pressure from the United States to halt their backing of the organization. It is reasonable to assume that prolonged American pressure on these two countries will have a significant effect on the organization's actions in upcoming years.[99]

CHAPTER 8

PALESTINIAN TERRORISM:
FROM NATIONALISM TO RELIGIOUS FUNDAMENTALISM

At the beginning of 1982, Israel invaded and occupied southern Lebanon and essentially put an end to the efforts of Palestinian terror organizations to establish their foundations there. Not only did this eliminate Palestine's military infrastructure in Lebanon, but it also led to a steady decline in Palestinian terror activities. In effect, in the mid-1980s, it appeared that the violent Palestinian struggle was gradually diminishing and that the Palestinian aspiration to achieve independent statehood was losing its chances of being accomplished.

In the second half of the 1980s, however, it became clear that this assumption was premature, especially once the (first) Palestinian Intifada broke out. *Intifada* is a general term for Palestinian violent acts of protest in the territories of Judea, Samaria, and Gaza, which took place between 1987 and 1992. Its onset seemed to be unplanned.

On Tuesday afternoon, December 8, there was a serious traffic accident in the Gaza Strip, as an Israeli truck driver made a sharp turn and struck a car filled with Palestinians, killing four passengers. Rumors spread throughout the Gaza Strip and the territories that the collision was not an accident but rather an act of vengeance for the murder of Israeli citizen Shlomo Sakal, which occured in the central market in Gaza two days before.[100] In any case, the result was a flare-up of mass rioting, at first mainly in the refugee camps in Gaza, but later also in the major cities of Judea, Samaria, and the Gaza Strip. In the first few weeks, the Intifada consisted primarily of a series of mass protests in which thousands of Palestinians, including women, children, and elderly people, took part. They threw rocks, burned tires in the streets, set up roadblocks, and engaged in other disturbances and breaches of the peace. In the years that followed, though, the Intifada also consisted of acts of terror against Israeli citizens and soldiers.[101]

The eruption of the Intifada signified a substantial change in the nature of the Palestinian struggle from a number of perspectives. For the first time, the Palestinian struggle was now waged inside Israeli territories. Also for the first time, the Palestinian population became increasingly influential and soon led the struggle. The most central change brought on by the Intifada, however, was the emergence of religious-fundamentalist Palestinian terror in the form of two groups—Hamas and Palestinian Islamic Jihad (PIJ).

The establishment of these two organizations and their transformation into the most dominant terror organizations in the area during the 1990s essentially signaled a change of the guard in Palestinian terror. On one hand, there was the ascendance of religious fundamentalist terrorism, and, on the other, there was the decline of leftist organizations (the various "fronts") and secular nationalist terror from the older school of

Fatah. Islamic Jihad and Hamas called for the annihilation of Israel in the name of Islam and, only afterward, in the name of a Palestinian identity. In effect, both organizations featured a two-pronged ideology: In the short term, their goal was the liberation of the Palestinian people and the establishment of an independent state. In the long run, these organizations sought to establish a Palestinian political entity that not only would be independent but also would be based on Islamic laws as part of a Pan-Arabic Islamic entity.

HAMAS

"Allah is the goal, the prophet is the sign, the Koran is the law, the jihad is the way, and death in the name of God is the most sublime wish." This sentence is the essence of Hamas's ideological platform, codified in the Hamas Covenant. The Hamas movement was first conceived by Sheikh Ahmed Yassin in 1978 as a registered association under the name Al-Mujamma Al-Islami and became known by its present name on the eve of the outbreak of the Palestinian uprising at the end of 1987. The main goal of Hamas, which in effect was a Palestinian incarnation of the Muslim Brotherhood, is to integrate the Palestinian nationalist project with the struggle to establish a united Islamic regime all over the Arab world. According to the Hamas movement, Palestine is a Muslim holy area whose sanctity is indisputable and unnegotiable, and therefore it is essential to "save it" from "Jewish infidels."[102]

Hamas has made use of both religious preachings and social welfare initiatives to widen its base of support. It was more popular in the Gaza Strip than the West Bank, given the large number of refugees there, the economic hardships of the population in the refugee camps, and the relatively low status of nationalist views. Indeed, Hamas has been successful in forming its own social welfare system, which has provided an alternative to the social-political structure of the PLO. Its prestige was and is based on both its ideological and practical capabilities; Hamas is a movement whose contributions to the daily life of Palestinians is no less important than its contribution to the armed struggle against Israel and the occupation.

Hamas embarked on the path of terror after the beginning of the First Intifada.[103] A great deal of Hamas's activities at that time included shootings and roadside bombs aimed at Israeli army patrols, as well as kidnappings of Israeli soldiers and civilians. For example, Hamas made a name for itself among the Israeli public after members abducted and killed two IDF soldiers, Avi Sasportas and Ilan Saadon, in January and May 1989, respectively, mostly because the families' struggle to locate their loved ones gained widespread media coverage.[104] Hamas also set its sights on civilian targets; for example, the sabotage of a Jerusalem restaurant in June 1990 (an incident that miraculously ended with no casualties), the detonation of a bomb in an absorption center (a place where new immigrants to Israel reside while they to find employment, housing, and study Hebrew) in the city of Hadera, and the explosion of a remote-controlled bomb in the middle of Jerusalem in July 1990 that caused three casualties.[105] Israel's tolerance of Hamas's actions reached its limits after organization activists killed an Israeli police officer in December 1992. The government of Israel subsequently decided to deport 415 Hamas activists to southern Lebanon.[106]

The expulsion of these members not only did no harm, but it in fact won the movement broad sympathy among the Palestinian population and the Arab world. The majority of those expelled returned to Israel in the following years and became prominent leaders of the organization. More important, during their time in Lebanon, they had the opportunity to get into contact with Hezbollah activists and improve the professional level of their methods of action. In the following years, this training process would find its practical implications in the massive suicide terror campaign mounted by Hamas against Israel.

PALESTINIAN ISLAMIC JIHAD

Palestinian Islamic Jihad (Harakat al-Jihad al-Islami al-Filastini) was founded in 1979 by Palestinian students in Egypt who had broken away from the Palestinian Muslim Brotherhood in the Gaza Strip. The founders were highly

Ahmed Yassin

The founder and a spiritual leader of the Hamas movement, Sheikh Ahmed Yassin was born in 1938 in the village of al-Jura, near the Israeli city of Ashkelon. After the war of 1948, his family fled to the adjoining Gaza Strip. When he was 12 years old, he was involved in a sports accident that left him disabled and confined to a wheelchair until his death. After having completed his studies, he became a teacher of Islamic religion and Arabic language, and was connected to various mosques in the Gaza Strip. During the 1970s, he became an extremist Islamic preacher, supporting the enforcement of Islamic principles throughout Israel, and founded an organizational network based on Islamic ideology that supplied humanitarian aid to the inhabitants of the Gaza Strip. Between 1983 and 1985, after trying to set up a military wing in his organization, he was jailed by Israel, charged with inciting to cause harm to the citizens and to the state of Israel. He was released in a prisoner exchange agreement and in 1987 officially established the Hamas (Islamic Resistance) movement in its present form. In 1991, he was again imprisoned and was given a life sentence. He was released in 1997 as part of an agreement between Israel and Jordan. This agreement came about in the wake of a failed Israeli attempt to assassinate the head of the Hamas political office in Jordan, Khaled Masha'al. In exchange for releasing the Mossad operatives who had been apprehended in Jordan during the assassination attempt, and in order to appease Jordan for the infringement of its sovereignity, Yassin was released. After his release, he continued to incite and to preach in favor of strikes at Israel and at Jews.

Sheikh Yassin was assassinated by Israeli Air Force helicopters on March 22, 2004, while leaving a mosque after early morning prayers.

Militant group's top leaders

Hamas secretly appointed a new Gaza Strip chief but refused to reveal his identity following the assassination of Abdel Aziz Rantisi.

Mahmoud Zahar, 53	**Ismail Hanieh,** NA	**Khaled Mashaal,** late 40s	**Moussa Abu Marzook,** early 50s
▶ Hamas spokesman and hard-liner	▶ Top aide to Yassin; ex-pelled to Lebanon in 1992	▶ Oversees Hamas' political bureau from Damascus, Syria; expelled from Jordan in 1999	▶ Mashaal's deputy in the political bureau
▶ Hamas founder Sheik Ahmed Yassin's personal physician; group's liaison with the PLO in the mid-1990s	▶ Member of Hamas' decision-making political bureau	▶ Helped negotiate a truce that temporarily halted Palestinian attacks on Israel	▶ U.S.-educated; detained by U.S. authorities in 1995 on suspicion of involvement in terrorism
▶ Opposes compromise with the PA	▶ Go-between with the PA	▶ Survived a poison dart attack in 1997 after Jordan's king coerced Israel into sending antidote	▶ Expelled to Jordan, then sent to Syria
▶ Imprisoned by Israel; jailed repeatedly by the PA	▶ Involved in efforts to work out an arrangement on how to run Gaza after an Israel pullback		

SOURCE: Associated Press   AP

Abdel Aziz Rantisi, Hamas's Gaza leader, was killed on April 17, 2004, by an Israeli missile strike. This graphic shows the group's top leaders, one of whom was appointed chief.

influenced by the Islamic revolution in Iran on one hand, and by the radicalization and militancy of Egyptian Islamic student organizations on the other. They also mounted terrorist operations inside Israel, mainly at the beginning of the first Intifada. Like Hamas, Palestinian Islamic Jihad founded a social support network, called Al-Dawa, comprising schools, kindergartens, and mosques.[107]

The first attack to be identified with the movement was the slaying of a yeshiva (a place where the Torah is studied) student named Aharon Gross in Hebron in August 1983. At the beginning of the Intifada, members of this movement played an extensive role in terror operations against Israel. Among the more well-known actions were the fatal stabbings of three Israelis (a police officer, a soldier, and a civilian) in October 1990 in Jerusalem and the planting of a bomb in the Mahane Yehuda Market in Jerusalem in May 1990, an incident in which one civilian was killed and nine were injured.[108]

PALESTINIAN TERRORISM IN THE 1990s AND THE NEW MILLENNIUM

The swell of the popular Palestinian uprising, set in motion toward the end of 1987, was finally subdued in 1993 when the Oslo Accords were signed between the PLO and the Israeli government. The Palestinian public, as well as its leadership, was split in its attitude toward the peace process with Israel. Opposed to the Fatah organization, which was chiefly responsible for the conciliation process with Israel, were a list of organizations (called the Refusal Front) headed by Islamic movements who categorically rejected the agreements. In a short while, the opponents to the agreements began to use terror measures in order to try and stop the peace process between Israel and the Palestinians. In addition, between April 1993 and August 1996, Hamas and the Islamic Jihad carried out 25 suicide attacks in many cities all over Israel, mostly striking at public transportation.[109]

The more outstanding attacks took place in Tel Aviv and Jerusalem, in crowded places and on buses. For example, on February 25, 1996, two suicide attacks were perpetrated by Hamas terrorists. The first was on a bus in Jerusalem that led to the deaths of 20 Israelis and 3 Americans and the injuries of 50 more civilians. The second was in the city of Ashkelon, in which a terrorist dressed up as an Israeli soldier—thus not provoking suspicion—approached a group of soldiers and set off an explosive device attached to his body. In this incident, 3 people were killed and 25 were wounded. On March 4 of that same year, another suicide bomber blew himself up at a major intersection in Tel Aviv on the day that the traditional Jewish holiday of Purim was celebrated. In the explosion, 14 were killed and 163 were wounded, many of them children. The entire campaign of suicide terror resulted in 211 people dead and 1,582 wounded.[110]

The aggressive Israeli counterresponse to Palestinian terror, together with international pressure put on the Palestinian Authority to take measures against terror organizations, led, to some degree, to a favorable outcome in 1998 and 1999, as the waves of suicide bombers slowly lessened. This letup was only temporary, however, and the eruption of the Second Intifada, the Al-Aqsa Intifada, toward the end of 2000, heralded the beginning of the most severe terror campaign that any democratic state had to endure in recent years.

The Al-Aqsa Intifada broke out following the visit of the leader of the Likud Party (the largest right-wing party in Israel) to the Temple Mount in September 2000. This visit was viewed by the Palestinians as a kind of challenge and provocation against them. Even before the visit, though, it seemed that the ensuing upsurge of violence was inevitable, especially since the peace process had reached a dead end, and it seemed that the patience and political leverage of moderates on both sides were no longer enough to prevent opponents of the peace process from taking action.

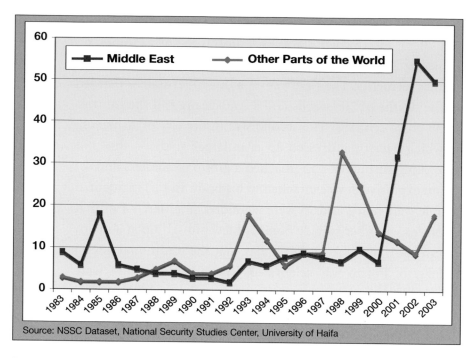

Source: NSSC Dataset, National Security Studies Center, University of Haifa

Figure 8.1 **This chart compares suicide attacks in the Middle East with suicide attacks in other parts of the world, by year.**

In the weeks following the controversial visit, violence erupted at full steam. The Fatah organization (which was in command of the Palestinian Authority security forces) attacked Israeli targets using conventional methods of terror (mostly roadside shootings), and the Islamic groups resumed their suicide terror campaign against civilian targets in the heart of the major cities of Israel. Between September 2000 and December 2004, more than 153 suicide attacks were carried out against a multitude of Israeli civilian and military targets.[111]

Among the more daunting incidents were the attacks on the Park Hotel in the city of Netanya and on the Maxim Restaurant in Haifa. The former took place on March 27, 2002, the eve of the Passover holiday in Israel. A Hamas suicide terrorist made his way into the hotel, which was full of people dining and celebrating the holiday. The bomber detonated the explosives belt attached to his body, and 30 people were killed and dozens more injured in the huge explosion. The incident was called the Passover (Eve) Massacre or Seder Eve Massacre. One-and-a-half years later, a female suicide attacker, Hanadi Jaradat, a member of the Islamic Jihad, blew herself up at the crowded Maxim Restaurant, on the outskirts of the city of Haifa. The terrorist, a lawyer by profession, walked into the restaurant and ordered lunch. After she finished eating, she approached the middle of the restaurant and detonated the explosives belt on her body, killing 21 people and injuring 60 more.[112]

The Al-Aqsa Intifada brought home the fact that the Israeli–Palestinian struggle was entering a new phase. No longer was it solely a territorial-nationalist conflict; it was now also an interfaith battle. Yasser Arafat himself, the leader of the secular Palestinian nationalist movement, began to adopt religious motifs in his declarations during the course of this Intifada.

This change was particularly evident in Arafat's speech before the Arab Summit Conference on October 21, 2000, when he described the events of the Al-Aqsa Intifada in terms of an interfaith battle and called upon the Palestinian people to take up arms against the attempt to Judaize Jerusalem.[113] Borrowing from chapter 7 of the Hamas Covenant, Arafat declared, "The Day of Judgment will not come about until Muslims fight the Jews (killing the Jews), when the Jew will hide behind stones and trees."[114]

In the following years, the Fatah not only adopted the terminology of Islamic organizations but also their modus operandi. Beginning in January 2002, Fatah fighting brigades also began to carry out suicide attacks. Their first suicide operation took place on January 27, 2002, when a female suicide terrorist blew herself up in a Jerusalem shopping center, killing one person and injuring more than 120.[115] Further, the Fatah also began to adopt the organizational network structure of the Islamic organizations and to set up small, relatively self-governing cells (which were called the Al-Aqsa Martyrs' Brigade). These cells

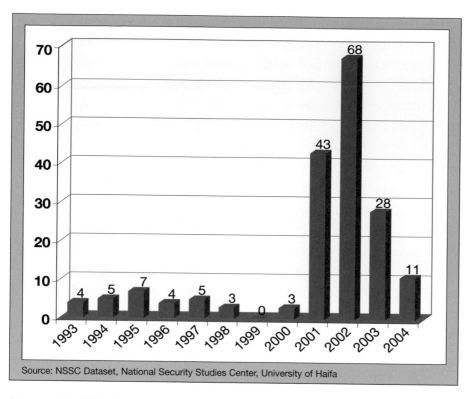

Source: NSSC Dataset, National Security Studies Center, University of Haifa

Figure 8.2 This bar chart illustrates the number of suicide attacks perpetuated by Palestinian organizations, per year.

were established in many Palestinian cities and functioned autonomously and according to their resources.

The Intifada is now entering its fifth year. With the death of Arafat in November 2004 and the election of Mahmoud Abbas (among the more moderate Palestinian leaders and a veteran opponent of the use of terror) to the head of the Palestinian Authority, once again there is a period of hope in which both sides will declare anew their intention to resolve the conflict without the use of violence and terror. This is only after (according to different sources) more than 3,500 Palestinians and 1,500 Jews have died and tens of thousands have been impaired for life, over the course of the Second Intifada.

CHAPTER 9

THE ASCENDANCE OF JEWISH MESSIANIC VIOLENCE

In contrast to the Jewish terrorism witnessed during the establishment of the state of Israel—terrorism with a goal of national liberation—the Jewish terrorism of the 1980s was the product of a "messianic" religious ideology. The majority of Jewish terrorists active in the 1980s were raised on the premises of the Gush Emunim movement. Members of this movement subscribed to religious Zionism—an offshoot of the Zionist movement, which sought to integrate Zionist-democratic and Jewish-religious values into the political process. The Gush Emunim movement considered the Six-Day War, in which Israel gained control over the majority of the Jewish holy places, a part of what they called the messianic "process of redemption." In their view, the eventual outcome would be the

Gush Emunim settlers and supporters celebrate the twentieth anniversary of Israeli control of the West Bank by marching around Jericho.

coming of the Messiah and the establishment of the Kingdom of Israel. The kingdom would be in strict accordance with the laws of the Torah and the Halakha and would lead to the restoration of Jewish sovereignty over all of the biblical Land of Israel. Accordingly, the people of Gush Emunim believed that settling on the lands of Judea and Samaria would help Israel gain control over the various parts of the Land of Israel and thus help accelerate the messianic process of redemption.[116]

Because of their messianic worldview, each time Israel became involved in a conciliatory process with an Arab country or the Palestinians, which of course would include relinquishing

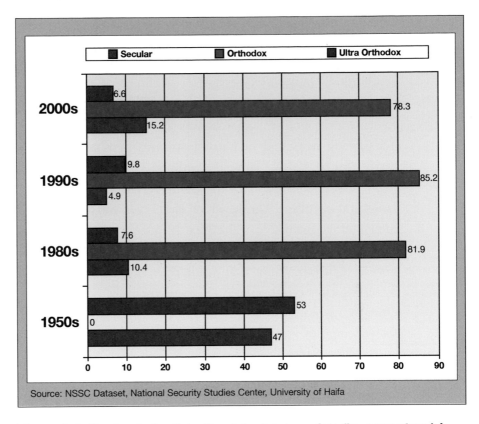

| | Secular | Orthodox | Ultra Orthodox |

2000s
- 6.6
- 78.3
- 15.2

1990s
- 9.8
- 85.2
- 4.9

1980s
- 7.6
- 81.9
- 10.4

1950s
- 0
- 53
- 47

Source: NSSC Dataset, National Security Studies Center, University of Haifa

Figure 9.1 The level of religiosity of Jewish terrorists (by percentage) is outlined in this graph. Note that in the 1950s, Jewish terrorists were either secular or ultra Orthodox. A half-century later, the majority of Jewish terrorists were Orthodox.

certain parts of the land of Israel, the Gush Emunim believers considered it a critical setback to the redemption of the people of Israel. Further, although most members of Gush Emunim opposed the various political processes by means of legitimate acts of protest, each time there seemed to be a chance of a political development that might include giving up some part of the land of Israel, there would also be a surge of activist and radical groups seeking to radicalize the types of action to which the movement traditionally subscribed. In other words, they would shift the focus of the ideological struggle of Gush

Emunim from mass protest and settlement activity (both legal
and illegal) to the use of systematic and organized violence
against different targets and especially against Palestinian
residents of Judea and Samaria.

The first Jewish terror group that intentionally attempted
to frustrate a political process was the Jewish Underground.
This group consisted of Gush Emunim members from the
territories of Judea, Samaria, and the Golan Heights, who
believed that the signing of the Camp David Accords between
Israel and Egypt in 1979 (in which Israel committed to and did
in fact return the whole of the Sinai Peninsula to the Egyptians)
was contrary to their ideals. They believed that a new group
needed to be established that would draw in the people of Israel
by setting a personal example and by performing radical actions.
Only in this way would it be possible to speed up the longed-
for redemption and defuse the processes hindering its arrival
(such as the Camp David Accords).[117]

The Jewish Underground planned for the climax of their
efforts to be the destruction of the Dome of the Rock Mosque
on the Temple Mount in Jerusalem. By doing so, they had
hoped to achieve two goals. First, they sought to undermine the
peace process between Israel and Egypt during the evacuation
of the settlements, knowing that damage to the third most
important symbol in the Islam religion would provoke an
eruption of violence and the annulment of the Camp David
Accords. Second, they believed this would also step up the
process of redemption by "clearing" the Temple Mount of
unwanted elements (the mosque was one of them) that were
hindering the construction of the Jewish Third Holy Temple
(necessary for redemption) in its place. Fortunately, this
scheme did not come to fruition, mostly because leaders of the
Jewish Underground were not able to obtain spiritual support
from their rabbis for this operation.

The Underground leadership understood that an operation of this kind demanded meticulous planning, the gathering

of operational experience, and a lengthy process of training. Therefore, at an early stage, the group decided to become better organized and to carry out retaliatory raids on the Palestinian population in Judea and Samaria, irrespective of the plot to destroy the Dome of the Rock Mosque on the Temple Mount.

The Underground's first operation took place in June 1980 and was a reprisal for the terror attack committed by Fatah activists, which had killed six yeshiva students in Hebron. The group intended to assassinate the mayors of five Palestinian cities in the territories, mostly because, as the Underground members saw it, these Palestinians were to blame for the deterioration in security in Judea and Samaria. The mayors were the representatives of terror organizations outside of Israel and were therefore directly responsible for the terror attack in Hebron. In the end, by planting explosive devices in the cars of the mayors, the Underground was able to injure two of them, as well as seven Palestinian civilians and one Israeli army sapper (a military detonation expert, who in this case was severely injured when he was summoned to defuse one of the bombs).

The Underground's second mission took place at the Islamic College in Hebron. Four of its militants stormed the college with gunfire and grenades, killing 3 students and wounding 33. In April 1984, members of the Underground were apprehended after they rigged five buses belonging to an Arabic travel agency with explosives in East Jerusalem. Fortunately, intelligence about the operation reached Israeli security forces before the bombs were detonated, allowing the devices to be defused and the Underground members imprisoned. Capturing members of the Underground and revealing their identities—they were among the elite of the Gush Emunim movement—came as a genuine shock for the Israeli public, most of whom were opposed to the Underground's terror actions.

Nevertheless, violence of varying degrees committed by radical settlers against Palestinian residents of the territories continued to occur on a regular basis. Mostly responsible for the incidents were rudimentary and loosely organized groups, such as the Committee for Security on the Roads.

According to its name, one may assume that the Committee for Security on the Roads was a passive security force. In actuality, though, the group initiated attacks against the Arab population in the mid- and late 1980s. Its members perceived the violence of the First Intifada as a civil revolution that could potentially endanger the control of Israeli authorities over the territories. In order to counter this danger, they launched systematic and violent acts against Palestinian Arabs. Usually, before they acted, they would gather information on police and IDF patrols, and if there were no security forces in the targeted

Religious Zionism

Religious Zionism is one of the ten streams that make up the Zionist movement. The group supports a combination of nationalism and religion. The ideological foundations of the movement maintain that the Jewish people, the Jewish religion, and the land of Israel are intrinsically connected, and that a form of Judaism that carries out all religious laws should be the major guiding principle for the Jewish nation in its land.

The most important spiritual leader of this movement in Israel was Rabbi Zvi Yehuda Kook (1891–1982), who considered settlement of the land of Israel as the beginning of the process of the redemption of the people of Israel (that is, a process that would lead to the establishment of a religious Jewish state). Even secular settlers were considered instruments in the advancement of this process. This stream of Zionism created its own religious educational system and has encouraged further religious settlement with the slogan "Work and Torah."

area, they would enter the Arab city in several cars and attack innocent civilians and burn cars and houses. The organizational structure of the committee was paramilitary, and it comprised almost 1,000 members.

After the signing of the Oslo Accords, another escalation in Jewish violence reached its peak in two outstanding incidents. The first was a massacre committed by Baruch Goldstein, a

The Oslo Accords

The Oslo Accords were agreements signed by the government of Israel and the recognized leadership of the Palestinian nation (that is, the Palestine Liberation Organization). These were intended to provide a nonviolent solution to the Israeli–Palestinian conflict.

Negotiations began in secret talks between an unofficial Israeli delegation of highly placed academics and others, and executive representatives of the PLO, such as Ahmed Qurei (Abu Ala) and Mahmoud Abbas (Abu Mazen), with Norwegian mediation. After this preliminary stage, official representatives of the two sides began secret talks to create a preliminary agreement to end the violent dispute between the sides and to set up the framework for independent Palestinian rule. At the end of August 1993, an agreement was initialed, and on September 13, it was officially signed at a festive ceremony on the White House lawn in Washington, D.C. In principle, the agreement determined that the first stage would consist of granting both military and civilian autonomy to the Palestinians in parts of the territories of Judea, Samaria, and the Gaza Strip, while accountability for other territories would be divided between the two sides but with full Israeli responsibility. The second part of the agreement, which was signed later, set a time frame for the establishment of a Palestinian state, alongside Israel, and an end to the dispute. When the Al-Aqsa Intifada broke out, many sections of the agreements became irrelevant.

Jewish settler, at the Tomb of the Patriarchs in Hebron. Goldstein stormed the holy place of worship with an automatic rifle and shot at Muslim worshippers, killing 29 and wounding more than 100. The other violent event was the assassination of the Israeli prime minister, Yitzhak Rabin, by a Jewish terrorist on November 4, 1995. The assassin, Yigal Amir, shot Rabin three times, just after Rabin finished speaking at a rally in support of the Oslo peace process. The gunman revealed in a later interrogation that in this way, he had wished to put an end to the peace process that Rabin himself had led with much resolve.

The assassination was not an isolated incident, however. In the long months preceding the killing, many Israeli right-wing and religious Zionist political and spiritual leaders made vilifying remarks against Rabin, some of which bordered on an outright call for his physical harm. For example, Moshe Peled, a member of parliament from the Israeli right wing, announced on August 30, 1993, "We are witness to an act of national treachery. When treason is committed, all rules and regulations are broken. The government has lost its legitimacy and therefore we will not accept any decision or agreement that bears its signature."[118]

Radical Jewish leadership in the United States spoke in a similar vein. Rabbi Kurtz, the head of the Chabad movement in Florida, stated in the middle of April 1995, "Rabin is tantamount to the enemy, and hence the rule, 'he who comes to kill you, make sure to kill him first,' applies to him."[119] The mid 1990s were therefore marked by the incitement of a segment of the Jewish public against the Rabin government policy, and mainly against the prime minister himself, in effect taking advantage of the freedom of expression in Israeli democracy. There were numerous manifestations of incitement, such as in the distribution of stickers that said "Kill Rabin," or in the displaying of posters of Rabin in a Nazi uniform during a right-wing demonstration in October 1995.[120]

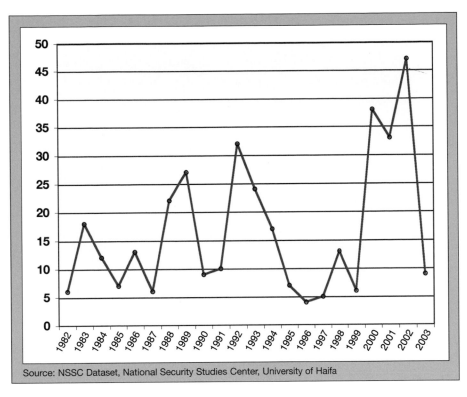

Source: NSSC Dataset, National Security Studies Center, University of Haifa

Figure 9.2 This graph shows the number of Jewish terrorist attacks in Israel, from 1982–2003.

At the beginning of the present millennium, security forces were still flushing out attempts to form Jewish terror groups. In September 2003, three Jewish residents of the settlement Bat Ayin were convicted on charges of attempted murder and the illegal bearing of arms. In April 2002, they had been caught hauling a wagon full of explosives and gas cylinders toward a girls' school in the East Jerusalem neighborhood of A-Tur.

At the end of July 2004, Jewish terrorists were still trying to sabotage conciliatory processes by violent means. The head of Israeli internal intelligence (the General Security Service) announced he had information regarding radical Jewish activists who were planning to blow up the Al-Aqsa Mosque in Jerusalem. Just a few days later, the Israeli minister of internal security announced he knew for a fact that, for the same reason, Jewish militants were planning to assassinate Ariel Sharon, the Israeli prime minister, though no such attempt was ever successful.

CHAPTER 10

AL QAEDA AND TERRORISM IN IRAQ

During the 1980s, Soviet armed forces waged a long, tough war against the Afghan Mujahideen. In 1989, the Soviets retreated from Afghanistan[121]—a decision that determined the fate of the pro-Soviet regime in Afghanistan. Indeed, just three years later, an extremist Muslim regime had replaced it.[122]

At the end of the war, the "Afghan graduates," now battle veterans and experienced fighters, began to return to their countries of origin—Algeria, Egypt, Tunisia, and Yemen. Several organizations in Afghanistan continued to maintain the operational and logistic infrastructure they had constructed during the war. One of these organizations was Qaedat al-Islam (Base of the Islam), more commonly known as al Qaeda, which was established by Saudi Arabian millionaire Osama bin Laden in 1988.[123]

Al Qaeda was essentially spawned on the wave of religious fervor that spread through the Middle East after the Islamic revolution in Iran and the Soviet invasion of Afghanistan, both in 1979. Deeply inspired by the revolution in Iran, bin Laden moved to Afghanistan directly after the Soviet invasion, raised money for Muslim fighters, established al Qaeda in 1988, and set up training camps for recruits.

At the end of the war, bin Laden returned to Saudi Arabia; however, he was forced to leave the country after openly protesting against Saudi Arabian collaboration with the United States during the Persian Gulf Crisis in 1991. Following a short stay in Sudan, bin Laden returned to Afghanistan in the mid 1990s and found refuge with the Taliban, who were in control of the country at that time.[124]

The Taliban movement emerged in 1994, out of the chaos that reigned in Afghanistan after the fall of the pro-Soviet regime in 1992. The founders of the Taliban movement were students of Islamic religious studies whose professed goal was not to accumulate power and strength, but rather to change the face of society entirely and subordinate it to the dictates of the Sharia (Islamic religious law).[125] In the first few months, the Taliban gained the support of the Kandahar residents by offering law and order in a region where chaos had governed for almost 20 years. Gradually, the movement extended its control to other regions in Afghanistan, taking advantage of the disputes between the administration of Burhanuddin Rabbani, leader of the country, and the forces opposing the regime. In October 1996, the movement instituted a nationwide radical Islamic government.[126]

When the Taliban regime conquered the cities of Kabul and Jalalabad, bin Laden began to devise the ideological anti-Western foundations of his organization. Bin Laden declared that Muslims must promise that only Allah is to be worshipped and, therefore, a violent war to the end must be fought against all infidels. He stressed the necessity to fight mostly against the Americans and their allies and concluded that they must be killed without distinguishing between civilians and fighters.[127] Al Qaeda's main objective was to undermine Western influence over the Middle East and in this fashion prevent the processes of modernization that went hand-in-hand with it. Western influence and modernization have been regarded by bin Laden as key obstacles to Islamic forces enforcing religious government throughout the Arab world.

In effect, though, the organization had already begun to operate against Western targets years before. In 1992, al Qaeda members set off an explosive device in a hotel in Yemen, where American soldiers customarily stayed. A year later, the group launched what they planned to be a mass attack on the World Trade Center in New York City. In that operation, al Qaeda activists exploded a car rigged with more than a half-ton of dynamite, gas cylinders, and acid, adjacent to the building's north tower. The terrorists' plan, masterminded by Ramzi Yusuf, one of the more prominent Afghan veterans, was to collapse the tower onto its southern twin at rush hour, when many people would be present. In addition to injuries and losses of lives, damages of about half a billion dollars were estimated to have been sustained in the explosion.[128]

On August 7, 1998, at 10 A.M., a massive explosion rocked the building that housed the U.S. Embassy in Nairobi, the capital of Kenya. A car carrying about 1,650 pounds (750 kilograms) of dynamite, driven by two suicide bombers, had exploded. As a result, 213 people were killed and 4,000 wounded.[129] On the same day, another car bomb loaded with about 550 pounds (250 kilograms) of dynamite exploded outside the U.S. Embassy in Tanzania. In this attack, 11 were killed and 85 wounded.[130]

The attacks on the American embassies in Africa were the last straw for the American administration. In the wake of these severe attacks, the United States bombed five bases of the al Qaeda organization in Afghanistan, as well as a factory for medication in Khartoum (the capital of Sudan), where, according to the Americans, materials for chemical warfare were being manufactured for bin Laden and his operatives. It seemed that this retaliatory action had no effect on al Qaeda's motivation to pursue its anti-Western objectives, however. Moreover, the group continued to enjoy Taliban patronage.

The attacks of September 11, 2001, were undoubtedly the most calamitous and significant blows in the chronicled history of terror to this very day. The attacks, in which four planes were hijacked and crashed, were the result of extensive scheming that was supervised by the headquarters of the al Qaeda organization in Afghanistan. As a result of these four crashes and the collapse of the twin skyscrapers, more than 3,000 people were killed, including citizens of 80 different countries.[131]

The four hijacked planes were apparently flown by 4 well-trained hijacker-pilots with the help of 15 others, all of them members of the al Qaeda organization and subordinate to the leadership and command of bin Laden. The organization assumed responsibility—albeit indirectly—for this unprecedented mega-attack in a cassette tape, where the organization's spokesperson, Suleiman Abu al-Ghaith, stated, "We have done the will of Allah . . . to support the oppressed and cast fear in the hearts of the infidels."[132]

The United States responded to the September 11 attacks with great force. It invaded Afghanistan and crushed the Taliban regime. Moreover, al Qaeda's operational infrastructures were eliminated and hundreds of militants were apprehended. Despite the heavy blow sustained to the operational and logistical infrastructure of the organization, al Qaeda attempted to resume its struggle by increasing its collaboration with other radical Islamic organizations. On October 12, 2002, a suicide bomber blew himself up inside a discotheque on the tourist island of Bali in Indonesia, taking the lives of 187 people. It turned out that the local Jemaah Islamiyah organization carried out the operation in conjunction with al Qaeda.[133]

A year later, four suicide bombers belonging to the Turkish Hezbollah attacked Western and Jewish sites in Istanbul. Investigations again revealed that al Qaeda had given the local organization logistic and operational assistance. The attack on the synagogues in Istanbul demonstrated that al Qaeda sought to include Israeli and Jewish targets in its list of enemies. A notable al Qaeda assault on an Israeli target took place on November 28, 2002, when an organization activist driving a jeep at 7:30 in the morning plunged through the security gate at the Paradise Hotel in the Kenyan city of Mombasa. Once inside, an individual exited the jeep, ran into the hotel reception area, and blew himself up next to a group of Israelis who had come to vacation there. Two passengers in the jeep detonated themselves and the vehicle at the same time. Altogether, 13 people were killed—3 Israelis and 10 Kenyans— and about 70 people were wounded. Several minutes after the attack, two shoulder missiles were launched at Arkia Flight 582, which had just taken off from Mombasa on its way to Israel. Fortunately, both missiles missed their target, an airplane carrying 271 passengers and crew. An investigation of the two attacks revealed that they had been engineered by Fazul Abdallah Mohammed, a high-ranking al Qaeda activist, who also was responsible for the attack on the U.S. Embassy in Kenya in 1998.[134]

At the beginning of the twenty-first century, it is possible to understand al Qaeda as an umbrella organization under which many terror groups operate to varying degrees. These groups appear in more than 45 countries around the world, including Pakistan, Iraq, Turkey, Saudi Arabia, Morocco, Indonesia, and others in the Middle East, Asia, and Europe. Many of these organizations view Osama bin Laden and al Qaeda as symbols and models for emulation and in fact tend to rally under their jihad rhetoric against the West.

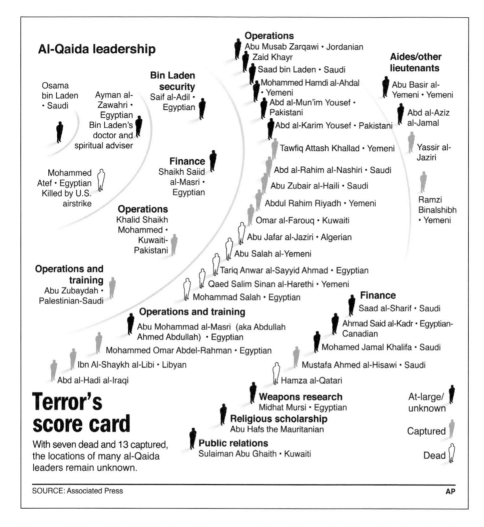

Al-Qaida leadership

Bin Laden security

Osama bin Laden • Saudi

Ayman al-Zawahri • Egyptian Bin Laden's doctor and spiritual adviser

Saif al-Adil • Egyptian

Operations
Abu Musab Zarqawi • Jordanian
Zaid Khayr
Saad bin Laden • Saudi
Mohammed Hamdi al-Ahdal • Yemeni
Abd al-Mun'im Yousef • Pakistani
Abd al-Karim Yousef • Pakistani

Aides/other lieutenants
Abu Basir al-Yemeni • Yemeni
Abd al-Aziz al-Jamal
Yassir al-Jaziri

Mohammed Atef • Egyptian Killed by U.S. airstrike

Finance
Shaikh Saiid al-Masri • Egyptian

Tawfiq Attash Khallad • Yemeni
Abd al-Rahim al-Nashiri • Saudi
Abu Zubair al-Haili • Saudi
Abdul Rahim Riyadh • Yemeni

Ramzi Binalshibh • Yemeni

Operations
Khalid Shaikh Mohammed • Kuwaiti-Pakistani

Omar al-Farouq • Kuwaiti
Abu Jafar al-Jaziri • Algerian
Abu Salah al-Yemeni

Operations and training
Abu Zubaydah • Palestinian-Saudi

Tariq Anwar al-Sayyid Ahmad • Egyptian
Qaed Salim Sinan al-Harethi • Yemeni
Mohammad Salah • Egyptian

Finance
Saad al-Sharif • Saudi

Operations and training
Abu Mohammad al-Masri (aka Abdullah Ahmed Abdullah) • Egyptian
Mohammed Omar Abdel-Rahman • Egyptian
Ibn Al-Shaykh al-Libi • Libyan
Abd al-Hadi al-Iraqi

Ahmad Said al-Kadr • Egyptian-Canadian
Mohamed Jamal Khalifa • Saudi
Mustafa Ahmed al-Hisawi • Saudi
Hamza al-Qatari

Terror's score card

With seven dead and 13 captured, the locations of many al-Qaida leaders remain unknown.

Weapons research
Midhat Mursi • Egyptian
Religious scholarship
Abu Hafs the Mauritanian
Public relations
Sulaiman Abu Ghaith • Kuwaiti

At-large/unknown

Captured

Dead

SOURCE: Associated Press   AP

Figure 10.1 **This 2003 chart illustrates the status of al Qaeda's leadership at that time.**

As for the future al Qaeda and its affiliate organizations, it appears that as long as activists of the al Qaeda terror network feel that terror as a method remains a key tool in their struggle with the military, industrial, and financial power of the West, then it will still be a viable option. In other words, as long as terrorists find this tool effective, they will probably continue to use it.

TERRORISM IN THE MIDDLE EAST OVER THE LAST TWO DECADES

There are very few states in the Middle East that have not suffered from terrorism. In addition, the states that have suffered most are those that are perceived to be the most powerful and that are considered to have the strongest armies, especially Egypt and Israel. This demonstrates one of the basic assumptions accepted by most researchers of terror: The use of terror tactics generally characterizes struggles that are not symmetrical, when it is clear to the weaker side that conventional violent struggle has no chance of success. To a great extent, it is still true to say that terror is the weapon of the weak.

Who can explain, then, why there is not one state in the Middle East that has not been connected to some form of terrorism—either struggling against terror, carrying out acts of terror, indirectly supporting terror, or financing terror? It is clear that the answer to this question is complex and the present discussion is not broad enough to deal with this complicated issue. Nevertheless, we can point out a number of factors. First, most states in the Middle East are young and are still in the process of establishing their forms of government, which leads to a large number of internal political struggles, often resulting in terrorism. Second, the Israeli–Palestinian dispute, as well as the fact that Israel is a strong military power with Western orientation in a Muslim area that, for many years, was oriented toward the Soviet Union, has led to much conflict. Power between Israel and both the Palestinians and the other Arab states has not been balanced, and this has led the Palestinians and those states that support them to turn to tactics of terrorism. Third, most states in the area are governed by regimes that are not democratic, and this has increased their potential to give refuge to a variety of terrorist organizations. In addition, it has facilitated the use of terrorism by the regimes themselves in order to achieve political goals or to eliminate their enemies.

It seems clear that although the Middle East is a geographically small and relatively homogenous area, it is the site of so

Religious and political divides

Iraq has long been a religious, ethnic and ideological mix. The Shiite Muslim Arabs are the majority, but Sunni Muslims are in power. Leaders of the Shiite opposition insist their share of power in any post-Saddam Iraq would have to reflect its majority, a position that worries other minorities as well as Iraq's mostly Sunni Arab neighbors.

*Christian presence

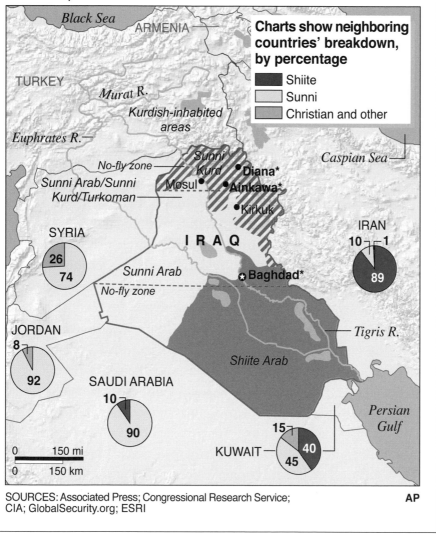

Charts show neighboring countries' breakdown, by percentage

■ Shiite
□ Sunni
▨ Christian and other

SOURCES: Associated Press; Congressional Research Service;
CIA; GlobalSecurity.org; ESRI   AP

Figure 10.2 This graphic shows the religious and political divisions in Iraq.

much terror activity that it has turned into a microcosm of the development of world terrorism. To a great extent, all of the international terror tactics have undergone upgrading and radicalization in the Middle East. This is true of hostage-taking for negotiation, suicide terrorism, political assassination, and other forms of terror.

The Middle East, as its name indicates, is a geographical area situated in a central geographic position. In the past and the present, it has been a focus of international interest because of its resources (oil, for example) and for its position at an important intersection, bordering the Mediterranean Sea, the Atlantic Ocean, the Red Sea, and the Indian Ocean. It is situated at the portal to Asia. Therefore, most of the important world powers have been interested in having influence in the area. The resulting involvement of most of these powers has led many terrorist organizations of the Middle East to operate against Western and other external targets.

What can we expect from Middle Eastern terrorism in the future? It appears that, despite the increasing involvement of the Western countries in the area, terrorism will continue to be an important tool in the political struggle between groups located there. However, not withstanding its wide dispersion throughout the area, it does not appear that terrorism will succeed in being an effective tool to achieve long-range goals. It seems clear that, to a great extent, the rise in the intensity of terrorism actually intensifies the power of the reactions against it rather than forcing the target countries to accept terrorist demands—thus making terrorism increasingly less effective.

Chapter 1
Defining Terrorism

1 Eyal Ziser, *Lebanon*. Kfar Kasm, Israel: Kfar Kasem Publications, 1993, p. 38 (Hebrew).

2 David B. Ottaway, "Sheik with Iranian Ties Is Suspect in Bombings," in the *Washington Post* (October 28, 1983): p. A 25; Robert Fisk, "What Drives a Bomber to Kill the Innocent Child?" in *The Independent* (August 11, 2001): p. 3.

3 According to the National Memorial Institute for the Prevention of Terror (MIPT) Database. http://www.tkb.org/Home.jsp.

4 Eli Karmon, *Coalitions of Terrorist Organizations 1968–1990*. Dissertation. Haifa, Israel: Haifa University, 1996, p. 87 (Hebrew).

5 Ibid., p. 278.

6 Bruce Hoffman, *Inside Terrorism*. New York: Columbia University Press, 1998, p. 38.

7 Ahmad Yusef alTal, *The Terror in the Arab and the Western Worlds*. Amman, Jordan: D.N., 1998, p. 13.

8 Jonathan R. White, *Terrorism*, 3rd ed. Belmont, CA: Wadsworth Thomson Learning, 2002, p. 5.

9 Boaz Ganor, *Defining Terrorism: Is One Man's Terrorist Another Man's Freedom Fighter?* Vol. 4. Herzliya: The Interdisciplinary Center, 1998, p. 12.

Chapter 2
First Seeds of Islamic Terrorism: Egypt and Syria

10 Bernard Lewis, *The Middle East: A Brief History of the Last 2000 Years*. New York: Schribner, 1995, p. 372; Yap, *The Near East*, p. 181.

11 Yap, *The Near East*, pp. 53–54.

12 David Sagiv, "Ideology of the Jihad Organizations in Egypt," in Jacob M. Landau, ed., *The New East: Journal of the Israel Oriental Society*, Vol. 36. Jerusalem: The Magnes Press, The Hebrew University, 1994, p. 135.

13 Yap, *The Near East*, p. 55.

14 William Spencer, *Islamic Fundamentalism in the Modern World*. Brookfield, CT: The Millbrook Press, 1995, p. 43.

15 Lacouture, *Nasser*, p. 86.

16 Ehud Yaari, *Egypt and the Fedayeen: 1953–1956*. Givaat Haviva: Center for Arabic and Afro-Asian Studies, 1975, p. 9.

17 Nssc Dataset. http://nssc.haifa.ac.il/.

18 Yap, *The Near East*, p. 177.

19 Amir Taheri, *Holy Terror: The Inside Story of Islamic Terrorism*. London: Huchinson, 1987, p. 175.

20 Israel Altman, "Islamic Opposition Organizations in Egypt," in Ami Ayalon, ed., *Regime and Opposition in Egypt* (Tel Aviv: TA University, 1983), p. 115 (Hebrew).

21 Altman, "Islamic Opposition Organizations in Egypt," p. 130.

22 MIPT Dataset. http://www.tkb.org/Home.jsp.

23 Eyal Zisser, *Faces of Syria: Society, Religion and State*. Tel Aviv: Hakibbutz Hameuchad, 2003, p. 252.

24 Yap, *The Near East*, p. 219.

25 Zisser, *Faces of Syria*, p. 248.

26 Moshe Maoz, *Syria*. Jerusalem: Office of Education, 1992, pp. 8–9.

27 Maoz, *Syria*, p. 10.

Chapter 3
Palestinian Terrorism: The National Secular Phase

28 Baruch Kimmerling and Joel S. Migdal, *Palestinians: The Making of a People*. Jerusalem: Keter, 1999, pp. 14–15.

29 Kimmerling and Migdal, *Palestinians,* pp. 147–149.

30 Danny Rubinstein, *Arafat: A Portrait.* Ganei-Aviv, Israel: Zmora-Bitan Publishers, 2001, pp. 63–64 (Hebrew).

31 Yap, *The Near East,* pp. 251–253.

32 Guy Bechor, *Lexicon of the PLO.* Tel Aviv: Ministry of Defence, 1995, p. 276.

33 Moshe Schwartzboim, *Arabic and Islamic Terrorism.* Haim Opaz, ed. Jerusalem: Office of Education, 1994, p. 5 (Hebrew).

34 Bechor, *Lexicon of the PLO,* p. 146.

35 Haarez Dally Newspaper, 25.6.69 (Hebrew).

36 Haarez Dally Newspaper, 23.11.68 (Hebrew).

37 Yaari, Ehud, *Fatah.* Tel-Aviv, Israel: A. Levin-Epstein, 1970, p. 239.

38 Kimmerling and Migdal, *Palestinians,* p. 205.

39 Ibid., p. 207.

40 NSSC Dataset. http://nssc.haifa.ac.il/.

41 Ibid.

42 Ibid.

Chapter 4
Terrorism in Pursuit of National Liberation

43 Spencer, *Islamic Fundamentalism in the Modern World,* p. 73.

44 Ibid., p. 74.

45 Jonathan R. White, *Terrorism: An Introduction,* 3rd ed. Toronto: Thomson Learning, 2002, p. 113.

46 Martha Crenshaw Huchinson, *Revolutionary Terrorism: The FLN in Algeria 1954–1962.* Stanford, CA: Stanford University, 1978, p. 74.

47 Ronen, *Algeria,* p. 8

48 Bechor, *Lexicon of the PLO,* p. 34.

49 Joseph Kister, *The National Military Organization—1931–1948.* Tel Aviv:

The Ezel Museum, 1998, p. 4 (Hebrew).

50 See Kister, *The National Military Organization,* pp. 4–11.

51 See Kister, *The National Military Organization,* pp. 4–11.

52 Ibid.

53 Josef Heller, *Lehi: Ideology and Politics: 1940–1949.* Jerusalem: Zalman-Shazar Center, 1989, p.173 (Hebrew).

54 Heller, *Lehi,* p. 210.

Chapter 5
Terrorism in Iran and Afghanistan: The Seeds of the Global Jihad

55 Yap, *The Near East,* pp. 141, 146.

56 Ibid., pp. 148–149.

57 Shaul Shay, *The Axis of Evil: Iran, Hizballah and the Palestinian Terror.* Herzliya, Israel: The Interdisciplinary Center, 2003, pp. 208–209.

58 Ervand Abrahamian, *Radical Islam: The Iranian Mojahedin.* London: I.B. Tauris, 1989, p. 86.

59 David Menashri, *Iran in Revolution.* Tel Aviv: Tel Aviv University, 1988, p. 77.

60 Ibid., pp. 78, 80.

61 Mark Downes, *Iran's Unresolved Revolution.* Aldershot Hants: Ashgate, 2002, p. 114.

62 Shaul Shay, *The Endless Jihad: The Mujahidin, the Taliban, and Bin Laden.* Herzliya, Israel: The International Policy Institute for Counter-Terrorism, the Interdisciplinary Center, 2002, p. 49.

63 Ralph H. Magnus and Eden Naby, *Afghanistan: Mullah, Marx and Mujahid.* Boulder, CO: Westview Press, 1998, p. 76.

64 J. Bruce Amstutz, *Afghanistan: The First Five Years of Soviet Occupation.* Washington, D.C.: National Defense University, 1987, pp. 40, 51.

65 Shay, *The Endless Jihad,* pp. 54, 56.

66 Peter Marsden, *The Taliban: War, Religion and the New Order in Afghanistan.* London and New York: Zed Books, 1998, p. 28.

Chapter 6
The Start of the New Middle Eastern Terrorism

67 Taheri, *Holy Terror,* p. 175.

68 MIPT Dataset. http://www.tkb.org/Home.jsp.

69 Ibid., pp. 20–21.

70 Ami Ayalon, *Egypt's Quest for Cultural Orientation.* Tel Aviv: The Moshe Dayan Center for Middle Eastern and African Studies, University of Tel Aviv, 1999, pp. 16, 37.

71 Shaul Shay and Yoram Schweitzer, *Afghanistan Graduates.* Erzlia, Israel: ICT, 2000, p. 7 (Hebrew).

72 Ayalon, *Egypt's Quest for Cultural Orientation,* p. 19.

73 Ami Ayalon. "Egypt Islamic Challenge," in David Menshari, ed., *The Fundamentalist Islam: Challenge for Regional Stability.* Tel Aviv: The Moshe Dayan Center, Tel Aviv University, 1993, p. 37 (Hebrew).

74 Ayalon, *Egypt's Quest for Cultural Orientation,* p. 20.

75 Shay and Schweitzer, *Afghanistan Graduates,* p. 8.

76 Spencer, *Islamic Fundamentalism in the Modern World,* p. 10.

77 Ayalon, "Egypt Islamic Challenge," p. 36.

78 Yap, *The Near East,* p. 379.

79 Ibid.

80 Rohan Gunaratna, "Suicide Terrorism: A Global Threat," in Pamala L. Griset and Sue Mahan, eds., *Terrorism in Perspective.* Thousand Oaks: Sage Publications, 2003, p. 221; MIPT Dataset. http://www.tkb.org/Home.jsp. http://www.tkb.org/Home.jsp.

81 Shay and Schweitzer, *Afghanistan Graduates,* p. 9.

Chapter 7
Sponsors of Terrorism: Syria, Iran, and Hezbollah

82 Ibid., pp. 256–257.

83 Yap, *The Near East,* p. 263; Maoz, *Syria,* p. 176; and Zisser, *Faces of Syria,* p. 259.

84 Hoffman, *Inside Terrorism,* p. 27.

85 Basar, *The Terrorism Dossier and Syria,* p. 21.

86 Ibid., pp. 63–64.

87 Eyal Zisser, *In the Name of the Father: Bashar alAsad's First Years in Power.* Tel Aviv: University of Tel Aviv, 2004, p. 182.

88 David Menashri, "Islamic Iran Between Revolutionary Ideology and Nationalistic Interests," in David Menshari, ed., *The Fundamentalist Islam: Challenge for Regional Stability.* Tel Aviv: The Moshe Dayan Center, Tel Aviv University, 1993.

89 Shay, *Terror in the Name of the Imam,* p. 64.

90 Hoffman, *Inside Terrorism,* pp. 191, 193.

91 Shay, *The Axis of Evil,* pp. 147–149.

92 Ibid., pp. 114–115.

93 Shay, *The Red Sea Islamic Terror Triangle,* pp. 65–66.

94 Ibid., p. 13.

95 Alexander Bley and Noham Thorn, *Hezbolla.* Jerusalem: Ministry of Education, 2002, p. 28.

96 Ibid.

97 Amal Saad-Ghorayeb, *Hizbu'llah: Politics and Religion.* London: Pluto Press, 2002, p. 147.

98 Zisser, *In the Name of the Father,* p. 270.

99 Zisser, in Webman, "Syria, Lebanon and the Hizbollah," p. 69.

Chapter 8
Palestinian Terrorism: From Nationalism to Religious Fundamentalism

100 Zehev Schiff and Ehud Yaari, *Intifada.* Tel Aviv: Schoken, 1990, p. 12 (Hebrew).

101 Nssc Dataset. http://nssc.haifa.ac.il/.

102 Shaul Mishal and Avraham Sela, *The Hamas Wind: Violence and Coexistence.* Tel Aviv: Miskal, 1999, p. 71.

103 Shaul Mishal and Avraham Sela, *The Palestinian Hamas.* New York: Columbia University Press, 2000; Schiff and Yaari, 1990, p. 243.

104 Mishal and Sela, *The Hamas Wind,* p. 88.

105 Nssc Dataset. http://nssc.haifa.ac.il/.

106 Mishal and Sela, *The Hamas Wind,* p. 174.

107 Shaul Mishal and Avraham Sela, *The Palestinian Hamas: Vision, Violence and Coexistence.* New York: Columbia University Press, 2000; ICT Website. http://www.ict.org.il/ (Hamas page).

108 National Security Studies Center Dataset. http://nssc.haifa.ac.il/.

109 Kimmerling and Migdal, *Palestinians,* p. 254.

110 Nssc Dataset. http://nssc.haifa.ac.il/.

111 Ibid.

112 Ibid.

113 Yasser Arafat's speech in the Arab Summit. Al-Iyam. 22.10.2000 (Arabic). Similar expressions were made in Arafat's speech in the Convention of the Palestinian Workers. *Al-Hyat Al-Jadida,* 28.10.2001 (Arabic).

114 Hamas Covenant. http://www.yale.edu/lawweb/avalon/mideast/hamas.htm.

115 Nssc Dataset. http://nssc.haifa.ac.il/.

Chapter 9
The Ascendance of Jewish Messianic Violence

116 Ehud Sprinzak, "From Messianic Pioneering to Vigilant Terrorism: The Case of Gush Emunim Underground," in David Rapoport, ed., *Inside Terrorist Organizations.* London: Frank Cas, 1987, pp. 194-217.

117 Nahama Gal-Or, *The Jewish Underground in the 1980s.* Tel Aviv: The International Center for Peace in the Middle East, 1986, pp. 20–22 (Hebrew).

118 Michael Karpin and Ina Friedman, *Murder in the Name of God.* Tel Aviv: Zmora Bitan, 1999, p. 100.

119 Carmi Gillon, *Shin-Beth Between the Schisms.* Tel Aviv: Miskal, 2000, p. 316.

120 Karpin and Friedman, *Murder in the Name of God,* pp. 131-135.

Chapter 10
Al Qaeda and Terrorism in Iraq

121 Graham E. Fuller, *Islamic Fundamentalism in Afghanistan: Its Character and Prospects.* Santa Monica, CA: Rand, 1991, p. 31.

122 See Magnus and Naby, *Afghanistan,* p. 158.

123 Shay and Schweizer, *Afghanistan Graduates,* p. 13.

124 Pamala L. Griset and Sue Mahan, *Terrorism in Perspective.* Thousand Oaks: Sage Publications, 2003, p. 52.

125 Ahmed Rashid, *Taliban: The Story of the Afghan Warlords.* London: Pan Books, 2001, pp. 22–23.

126 Shay, *The Endless Jihad,* p. 83.

127 Magnus Ranstorp, "Interpreting the Broader Context and Meaning of Bin-Laden's 'Fatwa.'" *Studies in Conflict and Terrorism* 21 (1998): pp. 321–330;

"Jihad Against Jews and Crusaders" in http://www.fas.org/irp/world/para/docs/980223-fatwa.htm.; "Bin-Laden's Fatwa" in http://www.pbs.org/newshour/terrorism/international/fatwa_1996.html.

128 Shay and Schweizer, *Afghanistan Graduates,* p. 161.

129 Ahmed Rashid, *Taliban: Militant Islam, Oil and Fundamentalism in Central Asia.* New Haven, CT: Yale University Press, 2000, p. 134.

130 Shay and Schweitzer, *Afghanistan Graduates,* p. 128.

131 Shay and Schweitzer, *Afghanistan Graduates,* pp. 135–136.

132 Ibid., p. 147.

133 Tariq Ali, *The Clash of Fundamentalisms: Crusades, Jihads and Modernity.* London and New York: Verso, 2003, p. 390.

134 Shay, *The Red Sea Islamic Terror Triangle,* pp. 150–152.

Alexander, Yonah. *Behavioral and Quantitative Perspectives on Terrorism.* New York: Free Press, 1981.

Amstutz, J. Bruce. *Afghanistan: The First Five Years of Soviet Occupation.* Washington, D.C.: National Defense University, 1987.

Bahgat, Gawdat. "Iran and Terrorism: The Transatlantic Response." *Studies in Conflict and Terrorism* 22 (1999), pp. 141–152.

Bley, Alexander, and Noham Thorn. *Hezbollah.* Jerusalem: Ministry of Education, 2002.

Bodansky, Yosef. *Islamic Anti-Semitism as a Political Instrument.* Tel Aviv: Tamuz, 2000.

Fisk, Robert. "What Drives a Bomber to Kill the Innocent Child?" *The Independent.* August 11, 2001.

Fuller, Graham E. *Islamic Fundamentalism in Afghanistan: Its Character and Prospects.* Santa Monica, CA: Rand, 1991.

Gunaratna, Rohan. "Suicide Terrorism: A Global Threat," in L. Pamala Griset and Sue Mahan, eds., *Terrorism in Perspective.* Thousand Oaks: Sage, 2003.

Hoffman, Bruce. *Inside Terrorism.* New York: Columbia University Press, 1998.

Hutchinson, Martha Crenshaw. *Revolutionary Terrorism: The FLN in Algeria 1954–1962.* Stanford, CA: Hoover Institution Press, Stanford University, 1978.

Laqueur, Walter. *The New Terrorism.* Oxford, UK: Oxford University Press, 1999.

Lewis, Bernard. *The Middle East: A Brief History of the Last 2000 Years.* New York: Scribner, 1995.

Magnus, Ralph H., and Eden Naby. *Afghanistan: Mullah, Marx and Mujahid.* Boulder, CO: Westview Press, 1998.

Marsden, Peter. *The Taliban: War, Religion and the New Order in Afghanistan.* London and New York: Zed Books, 1998.

Mishal, Shaul, and Avraham Sela. *The Palestinian Hamas: Vision, Violence and Coexistence.* New York: Columbia University Press, 2000.

Nussa, Andrea. *Muslim Palestine: The Ideology of Hamas.* London: Harwood Academic Publications, 1999.

Ottaway, David B. "Sheik with Iranian Ties Is Suspect in Bombings," *The Washington Post.* October 28, 1983.

Peleg, Ilan. "Terrorism in the Middle East: The Case of the Arab-Israeli Conflict," in *The Politics of Terrorism*, by Andreas Stohl. New York: Dekker, 1988.

Pluchinski, Dennis. "Middle Eastern Terrorist Activity in Western Europe: A Diagnosis and Prognosis." *Conflict Quarterly* 3 (1986): pp. 5–26.

Rashid, Ahmed. *Taliban: Militant Islam, Oil and Fundamentalism in Central Asia.* New Haven: Yale University Press, 2000.

Rashid, Ahmed. *Taliban: The Story of the Afghan Warlords.* London: Pan Books, 2001.

Saad Ghorayeb, Amal. *Hizba'allah: Politics Religion.* London: Pluto Press, 2002.

Sagiv, David. "Ideology of the Jihad Organizations in Egypt," *The New East: Journal of the Israel Oriental Society* 36 (1994): p. 135.

Springborg, Robert, and James, A, Bill. *Politics in the Middle East.* Boston: Little, Brown, 1999.

Sprinzak, Ehud. *Brother Against Brother.* New York: Free Press, 1999.

Wage, Carl, A. "Hezbollah Organization." *Studies in Conflict and Terrorism* 17 (1994): pp.151–164.

White, Jonathan R. *Terrorism: An Introduction.* Belmont, CA: Wadsworth/Thomson Learning, 2002.

Wilkinson, Paul. *Terrorism and the Liberal State.* New York: New York University Press, 1977.

Zisser, Eyal. *Faces of Syria: Society, Religion and State.* Tel Aviv: Hakibbutz Hameuchad, 2003.

Abu-Amar, Ziad. *Islamic Fundamentalism in the West Bank and Gaza: Muslim Brotherhood and Islamic Jihad.* Bloomington: Indiana University Press, 1994.

Becker, Jillian. *The PLO: The Rise and Fall of the Palestine Liberation Organization.* New York: St. Martin's Press (reprint ed.), 1985.

Burke, Jason. *Al-Qaeda: Casting a Shadow of Terror.* New York: I.B. Tauris, 2004.

Chasdi, Richard J. *Tapestry of Terror: A Portrait of Middle East Terrorism, 1994–1999.* Lanham, MD: Lexington Books, 2002.

Crenshaw, Martha. "The Effectiveness of Terrorism in the Algerian War," in Martha Crenshaw, ed., *Terrorism in Context.* University Park: Pennsylvania State University Press, 1995.

Cubert, Harold M. *The PFLP's Changing Role in the Middle East.* Portland, OR: Frank Cass, 1997.

Gunaratna, Rohan. *Inside Al Qaeda: Global Network of Terror.* New York: Columbia University Press, 2003.

Hussain, Asaf. *Political Terrorism and the State in the Middle East.* London: Mansell, 1988.

Iyad, Abou, and Eric Rouleau. *My Home, My Land: A Narrative of the Palestinian Struggle.* New York: Times Books, 1981.

Jaber, Hala. *Hezbollah.* New York: Columbia University Press, 1997.

Juergensmeyer, Mark. *Terror in the Mind of God.* Berkeley, CA: University of California Press, 2000.

Laqueur, Walter. *A History of Terrorism.* New Brunswick, NJ: Transaction Publishers, 2001.

Laqueur, Walter. *Voices of Terror: Manifestos, Writings and Manuals of Al Qaeda, Hamas, and Other Terrorists from Around the World and Throughout the Ages.* New York: Reed Press, 2004.

Mishal, Shaul, *The PLO Under Arafat: Between Gun and Olive Branch.* New Haven, CT: Yale University Press, 1986.

Rosaler, Maxine. *Hamas: Palestinian Terrorists* (Inside the World's Most Infamous Terrorist Organizations). New York: Rosen Publishing Group, 2002.

Ruwayha, Walid Amin. *Terrorism and Hostage-taking in the Middle-East.* France: S.N., 1990.

Sageman, Mark. *Understanding Terror Networks.* Philadelphia: University of Pennsylvania Press, 2004.

Yonah, Alexander. *Middle East Terrorism: Selected Group Profiles.* Washington, D.C.: Diane, 2004.

WEBSITES

Hamas Covenant
http://www.yale.edu/lawweb/avalon/mideast/hamas.htm

International Policy Institute for Counter-terrorism
http://www.ict.org.il/

The Middle East Media Research Institute
http://www.memri.org/jihad.html

The Middle East Review of International Affairs (MERIA)
http://meria.idc.ac.il/journal/2002/issue4/jv6n4a3.html

Middle East Studies Internet Resources
http://www.columbia.edu/cu/lweb/indiv/mideast/cuvlm/viol.html

National Memorial Institute for the Prevention of Terrorism (MIPT)
http://www.tkb.org/Home.jsp

Washington Report on Middle East Affairs (WRMEA)
http://www.wrmea.com/jews_for_justice/terrorism.html

page:

11:	Associated Press, AP	54:	Time Life Pictures/Getty Images
16:	© Kevin Fleming/CORBIS	62:	Associated Press, AP
18:	Associated Press, AP	72:	Associated Press, AP
27:	Associated Press, AP	80:	Time Life Pictures/Getty Images
32:	Associated Press, AP	84:	Associated Press, AP; ESRI
35:	Associated Press, AP	94:	Associated Press, AP
44:	Associated Press, AP		

ACKNOWLEDGMENTS

The research for this book entailed a long journey, during which I required and received a great deal of help. First, I would like to thank Ami Pedahzur, an excellent teacher and a dear colleague, who encouraged me to undertake this project. The book would not have been completed without his invaluable help and I would like to thank him from the bottom of my heart. I also would like to thank the National Security Studies Center at the University of Haifa and its head, Gabriel Ben-Dor, for all their support.

A wonderful group of young scholars were of vital assistance in the different stages of research for this book. Assaf Regev, a promising scholar, helped tremendously in gathering data about terrorism in the Middle East, especially that which occurred during the early years of the twentieth century. I am also grateful for the invaluable assistance of Adi Sela and Alexander Bialsky.

I had the honor and privilege of receiving advice and encouragement from Bruce Hoffman, Leonard Weinberg and Avraham Brichta—all offered me their wisdom and I am indebted to them for that.

As always, Dan Schlossberg, Olga Sagi, and Barbara Doron, wonderful editors, stood by my side, took very good care of the manuscript and made sure that my ideas would be communicated in a clear and coherent way.

Finally, I would like to thank Lily, Yotam, Naama, Elsa, and Amalia, whom I love so much.

ARIE PERLIGER is an adjunct faculty member at the School of Political Science at the University of Haifa in Israel, where he teaches undergraduate courses in terrorism and counterterrorism, Israeli politics, the extreme right in Europe and Israel, and political socialization and research methods. He is also a research fellow at the university's National Security Studies Center, where he is the coordinator of all political violence and terrorism studies as well the supervisor of the Center's terrorism datasets.

During the past four years he has published more than ten works in two main research fields: terrorism and political violence and the principal ways democratic states react; and the radical right and extremism. His publications focus mainly on suicide terrorism, Jewish terrorism and counter-terrorism. In June 2005 his first book, *Countering Terrorism in Jerusalem 1967–2002*, was published (with Ami Pedahzur and Gadi; Pahran-Jerusalem Institute Publications).

LEONARD WEINBERG is Foundation Professor of Political Science at the University of Nevada. Over the course of his career he has been a Fulbright senior research fellow for Italy, a visiting fellow at the National Security Studies Center (University of Haifa), a visiting scholar at UCLA, a guest professor at the University of Florence, and the recipient of an H. F. Guggenheim Foundation grant for the study of political violence. He has also served as a consultant to the United Nations Office for the Prevention of Terrorism (Agency for Crime Control and Drug Prevention). For his work in promoting Christian–Jewish reconciliation Professor Weinberg was a recipient of the 1999 Thornton Peace Prize.

WILLIAM L. EUBANK is a graduate of the University of Houston, where he earned two degrees (B.S. and M.A.) in political science. He received his Ph.D. from the University of Oregon in 1978. Before coming to the University of Nevada, he taught briefly at California State University Sonoma and Washington State University. While at the University of Nevada, he has taught undergraduate courses in Constitutional Law, Civil Rights & Liberties, Political Parties and Elections, and graduate seminars in American Politics, the History of Political Science and Research Methods. The author or co-author of articles and papers in areas as diverse as statistics, research design, voting, and baseball, among other subjects, he is interested in how political violence (and terrorism) function as markers for political problems confronting governments.